Eating to S

Food Choices fc

By Linda Riebel and Ken Jacobsen

CELESTIALARTS

Berkeley • Toronto

CELESTIALARTS
P.O. Box 7123
Berkeley, California 94707
www.tenspeed.com

Distributed in Australia by Simon and Schuster Australia, in Canada by Ten Speed Press Canada, inNew Zealand by Southern Publishers Group, in South Africa by Real Books, in Southeast Asia by Berkeley Books, and in the United Kingdom and Europe by Airlift Book Company.

Cover and Interior Design by Larissa Pickens.
Cover Photo by Robert L. Bugg: sustainable agriculture in practice, almonds and clover in Chico, California.

BC cartoon by permission of Johnny Hart and Creators Syndicate, Inc.
Mutts cartoons reprinted with special permission of King Feature Syndicate
Chefs' Collaborative statement of principles copyright 2000 Chefs' Collaborative.
Reprinted with Permission.
Pyramid diagram on page 85 reprinted by permission of the Ohio State University College of Food, Agriculture, and Environmental Sciences.

Library of Congress Cataloging-in-Publication Data
Riebel, Linda.
    Eating to save the earth : food choices for a healthy planet / by Linda Riebel, Ken Jacobsen.
       p. cm.
    ISBN 1-58761-116-3
    1. Food. 2. Human ecology.   I. Jacobsen, Ken, 1946-   . II.
Title.
    TX357 .R54 2001
    641—dc21
                                    2001006096
First printing, 2002
Printed in Canada
1 2 3 4 5 6 7 8 9 10 — 06 05 04 03 02

Acknowledgments

We would like to thank the people who read all or part of this book and gave information or suggestions: Allen Kanner, Pam and Roy Webb, John Kerwin, Michele Simon, Michele Vivas, Don Lindsay, Jeannine Cuevas, Andy Snow, Melanie Joy, Erik Marcus, Ruth Richards, Susan Kegley, and Susan Korte. Any errors that may remain are the responsibility of the authors.

We also thank our supportive friends Brad Wade, Benny Juarez, Linda Brubaker, Ione Byrnes, and Jane Kaplan.

Tom Southern, our editor, gave contructive suggestions every step of the way.

for Peter Huntley Snow

Contents

Part Three: Away from Home   59

Part Four: Food for Thought   73

Preface

You can help save the earth. You don't need to petition, march, write letters to Congress, or invent an energy-saving device, though those are worthy activities, too. You can help the earth every time you shop and eat.

Unless you are in a dorm, barrack, convent, or prison, you spend thousands of dollars a year on food. In 1996, each American's food consumption amounted to $2,605 per year. Every dollar you spend can support earth-friendly foods and minimal packaging. As business guru Paul Hawken says, "The cash register is the daily voting booth in democratic capitalism." This book shows you how to make your votes (all 2,605 of them) count.

We believe that

- Making conscious food choices is a powerful and effective way to help the planet.
- Every individual counts.
- The ranks of environmentally responsible people are growing.

Every day, more Americans are deciding to put their environmental values into action. One researcher found that 24 percent of the adult population, or 50 million Americans, are actively concerned about social and environmental causes. Other researchers call them the New Green Mainstream. So you're not alone. People in many walks of life are inventing an amazing range of environmentally creative ideas. Schoolchildren are sending money to save rain forests, architects are designing energy-efficient homes and offices, religious communities are adopting environmental causes, and manufacturers are streamlining their processes. Exciting developments are taking place all around us.

In the world of food, farmers are reviving or developing earth-friendly techniques. Creative cooks are dreaming up delicious baked and frozen meatless foods. Organic produce is becoming easier to find. Restaurant chefs are protecting endangered species. Over 3,600 natural grocery stores sell earth-friendly items. Even grocery chains stock vegetarian and organic foods. You can also order them online.

How can changing your eating habits make a difference? Food is a huge segment of the American economy, amounting to $885 billion in 1999. This was almost 9 percent of the gross domestic product. Americans spend more on food than the total gross domestic product of many countries. We spend more on food than on our military budget.

Your share of this cornucopia depends, of course, on your circumstances. Are you on a tight budget or feeding a young family? Then you might be spending your food dollars on pasta and peanut butter, with only the occasional splurge. Are you a business executive who takes colleagues out on expense-account meals to fine restaurants several times a week? Your food dollars are spent very differently. With so many possible lifestyles, there's no average food style. But anyone, of any age or social group, with any combination of needs and preferences, can make food choices that help the earth.

This book gives you many options. You can choose which and how many choices to make. You can decide how much you want to know about each choice. (There are a few facts on each page, longer essays in the back, and resources for further reading.)

You can decide in what order to read the sections, and you can respond and contribute by visiting our web site *www.savenature.org/food*.

Introduction

Our planet faces many dangers—global warming, ozone thinning, rain forest destruction, water and air pollution, species extinctions, and topsoil depletion, to name a few. Our food choices have an impact. The way we grow food is part of the problem. We use so much machinery, pesticides, irrigation, processing, and transportation that for every calorie that comes to the table, 10 calories of energy have been expended. Experts once found that a 5-calorie strawberry was flown to New York at a cost of 435 calories of energy.

Food also causes other problems: 15 metric tons of soil are lost annually to feed each US resident because our agricultural practices erode soil. This amounts to 2 billion tons of soil a year. Almost 40 percent of the world's agricultural land is seriously degraded. Modern agriculture causes about one quarter of the risk of climate change.

Another danger is the quantity and kind of foods we choose. We eat too much—contributing to an alarming rise in obesity. Restaurant portion sizes have increased, in some cases by 100 percent. More restaurants are serving gigantic portions. One restaurant in Texas offers a meal of a 72-ounce steak plus shrimp cocktail, potato, salad, and bread. The meat industry is the second largest environmental threat. Only cars pose a greater risk. We overpackage food and expect to have out-of-season produce, which is grown thousands of miles away. Wild salmon and other fish are endangered from overfishing.

Recently, the Audubon Society reported that the earth could feed 10 billion people who eat as citizens of India do, 5 billion who eat like Italians, but only 2.5 billion who eat like Americans. According to Alan Durning, founder of Northwest Environment Watch, "The prospect of 5 billion people eating the way Americans do is an ecological impossibility, requiring more grain than the world can grow and more energy, water, and land than the world can supply."

Containing our population is obviously part of the solution. Changing our patterns of consumption is another part. This book will show you how your food choices can help the earth and yourself.

Your four most important decisions

Most of our recommendations boil down to four key decisions:

✓ Less meat, dairy, fish, and eggs

✓ Less processing, packaging, and waste

✓ More organic foods

✓ More diversity

You can decide which recommendations make the most sense for you. One person may make changes in three areas, while another may focus on one. If you decide to keep meat in your diet, you might change the kind and amount. If you're a vegetarian, you can reduce packaging and increase your purchase of organics. Let's look at each guideline in more detail.

Less meat, dairy, fish, and eggs

By far the heaviest burdens our diet places on the planet are meat and other foods of animal origin. Animals raised for food eat a large percentage of our grain crops, require millions of gallons of water, and give off waste that pollutes rivers, groundwater, and soil. Modern factory farming crowds animals into such unhealthy conditions that they need huge doses of antibiotics just to survive, and producers give them hormones to make them grow faster than nature intended. These chemicals enter our environment and our bodies, where some remain for long periods.

Add to this the damage to human health caused by a meat-heavy diet and the huge medical costs required to treat them. Cholesterol-heavy diets contribute to heart disease, atherosclerosis, stroke, and hypertension. Diets lower in animal products are the healthiest, according to Harvard University, the Physicians' Committee for Responsible Medicine, and the American Dietetic Association.

- Seven calories of vegetation are required to make one calorie of food of animal origin

- Leaks from hog waste cesspools pollute thousands of miles of river and kill millions of fish.

- 43 percent of managed species are overfished. The government has declared fishery disasters in Alaska, New England, and the West Coast.

Eating less food of animal origin is the single most powerful choice you can make for your health and for the earth.

Less processing, packaging, and waste

Millions of tons of natural resources go into processing, packaging, and transporting our food. Some packaging is necessary, but we make it worse by expecting perfect-looking produce, heavily packaged convenience foods, and out-of-season fruits and vegetables transported thousands of miles in gas-powered refrigerated trucks.

Processing is the work of cooking and assembling the product; adding coloring, additives, and preservatives; and shipping it from one plant to another, each time using gasoline and packaging and diminishing the product's natural nutrients.

Did you know that food in America travels an average of 1,300 miles before reaching the consumer? Some of our produce comes from as far away as Chile and Australia. We also export food: for example, midwestern beef goes to South Korea, and California broccoli goes to Japan.

Packaging wastes natural resources and creates garbage.

- In 1970, we used 72,700 tons of aluminum to make soda and beer containers; in 1990, we used 1,251,900 tons. Our aluminum consumption grew by a factor of 17 in only 20 years.

- Every day the United States generates 200 million tons of trash, or 4.3 pounds per person. This includes packaging used during manufacturing and distribution, waste that you don't personally create.

- Americans use 25 million plastic soda containers daily, created from 800 million pounds of virgin plastic.

Waste occurs at the farm, the factory, the store, and the kitchen.

- In Alameda County, California, businesses throw away 500,000 pounds of food every day.

- The typical household throws out 10-15% of the food it purchases.

- If 5 percent of wasted food were recovered, we would save $50 million a year in landfill costs alone.

When you eat more fresh, seasonal, local food, you lighten the burden on the earth. When you reduce your packaging, by buying in bulk, for example, you help reduce the number of trees cut down for paper, the amount of petroleum turned into plastic, the amount of minerals dug up to make aluminum —plus all the energy and oil required to run the factories that make the packaging. We'll show you ways to reduce waste so that your food stretches farther and ultimately returns to replenish the soil.

More organic food

Modern agriculture depends on chemicals: pesticides to kill insects, herbicides to kill weeds, antibiotics and hormones given to increase the bulk of animals sent to the slaughterhouses. Additives and preservatives are added to foods at the processing plant to make the food last longer and retain color or texture. Each meal you eat may contain only a small amount of these chemicals, but their impact can be cumulative over a lifetime.

Did you know we're using 33 times more pesticides than we were 50 years ago? Yet crop losses are 20 times greater. This is because the pests have become resistant to chemicals, evolving to survive them. Farmers, encouraged by chemical manufacturers, respond by putting yet more chemicals on their crops.

- According to the World Health Organization, 20,000 agricultural workers die a year because of exposure to chemicals, in addition to a million non-lethal poisonings.

- Nearly 1,000 pests have become resistant to pesticides at certain levels. Such resistance costs the U.S. $1.5 billion a year.

- Pesticide use is still going up. California has used 5% more per acre since 1994; in 1998, this amounted to 50 million pounds.

Agriculture experts call this trend the "pesticide treadmill." This situation reminds us of drug addiction. When people are addicted, they develop a need for ever-greater quantities of the substance in order to get the same effect. American agriculture seems to be addicted to chemicals.

Pesticides also disturb food webs. If we kill off most of one species, then the ones they used to feed on can multiply and become new pests. For instance, after certain pesticides were introduced on apple trees in northeastern United States, the European red mite, freed from its predator, became more prevalent.

Fortunately, organic farming is one of the fastest-growing segments of American agriculture, with sales growing 20-25% a year, now approaching $8 billion a year. If you eat more food grown with little or no chemicals, you can help shift our growing methods and help take poisons out of circulation.

More diversity

The health of an environment depends partly on how many different species live there—its biodiversity. When species are lost, whole webs suffer. When we eat species that are overexploited, we contribute directly to their decline and the decline of their food-chain neighbors. Other human activities, such as clear-cutting forests, also destroy ecosystem communities and threaten biodiversity.

- In 1994, 26,333 plant species and 5,929 animal species were classified as endangered or vulnerable.

- Almost one quarter of the world's mammal species and one eighth of bird species are threatened with extinction.

- The current extinction rate is 100 to 1,000 times the background or normal rate. The last major extinction on this scale occurred 65 million years ago.

- Worldwide, tropical rain forest cutting clears 35 million acres, leading to the loss of 14,000 to 40,000 species a year. We are losing rainforest area the size of Connecticut and Rhode Island annually.

We're putting all our eggs in a few genetic baskets. Three quarters of the world's food comes from seven crops—wheat, rice, corn, potato, barley, cassava, and sorghum. Unfortunately, the genetic diversity of these crops is rapidly disappearing: their native habitats are being destroyed and fewer varieties of each species are being cultivated. In this country, 90 percent of our eggs come from White Leghorn chickens, 70 percent of dairy cows are Holsteins, 96 percent of peas are from two varieties, and 40 percent of U.S. potato acreage is planted in Russet Burbanks.

Modern agriculture creates huge fields of a single crop. Those amber waves of grain are hundreds of acres of a single variety of a single species. This monoculture sounds sensible, bringing to farming the economy of scale and efficiency of movement that work so well in assembly line manufacturing. Unfortunately, it backfires in nature. Monoculture exhausts the soil, so farmers use more chemical fertilizers. Large stands of single crops attract pests with an inexhaustible supply of their favorite food. Science writer Janine Benyus calls monoculture an "all-you-can-eat restaurant for pests." In response, growers use more pesticides.

Meanwhile, 1,100 United States food species are endangered or threatened with extinction, not to mention those that have already disappeared. Since 1900, 6,000 apple varieties and 2,300 pear varieties have become extinct. Such losses can lead to inbreeding and genetic weakness in a species. When there are too few individuals of a species for it to survive with healthy diversity, it reaches what experts call a "genetic bottleneck."

Fortunately, heirloom seeds are being grown and propagated by dedicated individuals and groups, including Seed Savers, Native Seed Search, Of the Jungle, Seeds of Change, J.L.Hudson, and Seedsblum. Many people grow some of their own food and find it very satisfying. When you choose more diverse foods, you encourage farmers to grow them and help reverse the trend toward a genetic bottleneck.

"Biodiversity—the sum total of all the world's life forms, organisms, and genes—is nature's fail-safe mechanism against extinction... Any smart banker will recommend a diversified portfolio to hedge against a risk."

—Ecologist Kenny Ausubel

Time and money

You may be thinking, "How can I afford to save the earth? Who has the time or money?" People love the idea of saving the earth, but wonder how they'll find time and money to do it. Below we suggest things you can do, depending on whether you have more time, more money, or not enough of either.

You have more time than money

✓ Cook at home rather than eating at restaurants or buying convenience foods

✓ Brown bag your meals at work, school, or volunteer activities

✓ Grow your own food

✓ Use leftovers

✓ Compost the scraps

✓ Volunteer at an environmental organization

✓ Join a community garden

✓ Share extras with local food banks

✓ Avoid excess packaging

You have more money than time

✓ Buy organic foods

✓ Join a farm through community supported agriculture

✓ If you buy prepared and frozen food, choose vegetarian

✓ Patronize green restaurants

✓ Avoid excess packaging

Broke and busy—not enough time or money

✓ Learn one good soup or stew recipe for using leftovers

✓ Buy from earth-friendly producers

✓ Practice one of our suggestions at a time

✓ Spread the knowledge in this book to friends, family, coworkers, and members of your community

Citizen power

A single person or a small group has often changed the world. Many of us remember anthropologist Margaret Mead's remark: "Never doubt that a small group of thoughtful committed citizens can change the world. Indeed, it is the only thing that ever has."

In 1960, Catherine Kerr, Sylvia McLaughlin, and Esther Gulick noticed that development threatened the San Francisco Bay as landfill poured onto shorelines to be covered over by houses and roads. These three women and others got cities around the bay to restrict infill, preserving shorelines and the living waters of the bay. Today the area is one of America's most desirable places to live.

Surfers in California became concerned about pollution and degradation of beaches they loved. The Surfrider Foundation took the polluters to court and by the early 1990s won the second-largest Clean Water Act suit in American history. Today, the Surfrider Foundation, with 25,000 members and many overseas affiliates, also educates skiers and snowboarders about mountain watersheds.

Brothers Lee and Paul Heineman of Kansas City, Missouri, collected over 30,000 aluminum cans from local parks and parking lots, their parents' guests, the local senior center, and other adults they have recruited. The boys exchanged the cans for cash and sent the money to the Gorilla Foundation to help build a sanctuary in Hawaii. They're still collecting cans and sending money to endangered animal organizations such as World Wildlife Fund and the Jane Goodall Institute. Lee and Paul are ages eight and five.

Caring for the earth can bring together people who disagree on other things. The Green Scissors Coalition, for example, brings together environmental groups like Friends of the Earth with the conservative National Taxpayers Union to oppose ecologically damaging corporate projects. Anheuser-Busch recently agreed to stop pasturing cattle on some of its land because the cows were spoiling streams needed by trout. Pressure on home building giants Home Depot and Lowe's to stop buying unsustainable lumber contributed to a recent agreement to spare 3.5 million acres of Canada's old-growth forests. Citizens can boycott a destructive company and patronize ("buycott") a sustainable one.

Earth-savvy Americans

Millions of Americans are already moving toward earth-friendly lifestyles when choosing what to eat, what to wear, where to live, what car to drive, where to travel, and how to invest their savings. According to a Gallup poll in April, 2000, one in six Americans is active in the environmental movement, over half are sympathetic to it, and four-fifths are sympathetic to its goals. Over half would buy sustainably grown food if it is easy to find, tastes good, and doesn't cost too much. Other researchers found that if quality and price are equal, 76 percent of consumers would switch to a brand or retailer associated with a good cause.

In the food sector, we're buying organics more than ever before. In 1996, we spent $11.5 billion on natural products, including soaps and cleansers. The organic market is $8 billion a year, with annual growth of 20 to 25 percent. We're planning our shopping, as well. The Council on Economic Priorities, which reports on corporate behavior, has sold over 1 million copies of its consumer guide since 1988. And socially responsible investing in companies that have good labor, consumer, and environmental practices now amounts to over $2 trillion.

We've already made great strides in one area—recycling. By 1996, the United States had almost 9,000 recycling programs. The recycling rate almost tripled in the ten years between 1985 and 1995; in Minnesota, the recycling rate is an impressive 46 percent. In 1995, Americans recycled over 62 billion cans. The Union of Concerned Scientists observed, "The triumph of recycling is especially impressive because so much of the change in attitudes and individual behavior was instigated by seemingly powerless children and teenagers who prodded their families, schools, and colleges into action."

This widespread support of earth-friendly choices may come as a surprise. You may have thought people who care about the environment were just a few earnest activists holding meetings and criticizing other people's lifestyles. Or you may be an environmentally concerned citizen worried that there aren't enough like-minded people. How does this happen? Partly because the forces that work the hardest to get our attention—television, movies, and corporate advertisers—are not especially motivated to publicize environmental issues.

In fact, most big businesses are motivated to do the opposite. They make their money by extracting materials from the earth to turn into products to sell to you. They spend billions of dollars a year advertising to you, to make you discontented with what you have and insecure about who you are, and to convince you that happiness and popularity can be bought. The end result is consumerism, a.k.a. "affluenza," the constant spending that keeps us in debt but never quite happy.

Fortunately, the Internet is making it easier than ever to gather information, and get support for creative ideas that may not make lots of money for large interests. Mainstream publications are increasingly reporting on environmental issues with columns or entire sections on science, the environment, and consumer issues.

Every choice, even one made with good intentions, has consequences that may be hard to predict. There are trade-offs. For instance, coffee can be purchased in metal cans or in vacuum packs made of aluminum foil and plastic laminate. The can has 85 percent more material, but it's recyclable, so maybe that's the better choice. But if you compare the weight of the metal can with the weight of the foil, the foil seems like the better choice. For another example, you may choose organic milk, but it might be shipped a long distance. Still, we believe it's more important to take actions now that are probably good or that establish better habits than to wait for perfect solutions.

You may not agree with everything we suggest—we don't even always agree with each other! Ken eats meat and thinks biodiversity would be served if ostrich and buffalo flesh became common table items, while Linda is vegetarian and thinks the earth's resources should be used differently. But we agree that it's important to do what we can rather than argue over exact strategies or set impossible goals. There is so much need for change and so much room for creativity that we can all choose actions that will help.

Good news for the earth

There is reason to be cautiously hopeful about our future. People in many fields are inventing or reviving ways to live lightly on the earth, and citizens are buying and even demanding these goods and services.

At a coffee plantation in Hawaii, for example, geese are the only form of weed control. In addition to munching weeds, geese provide manure, which reduces fertilizer costs, recycles nitrogen, and creates soil to retain moisture. Since the owners put up a fence to keep out pigs and dogs, more ground-nesting birds such as wild turkeys and caliche pheasants can safely nest there. This tasty organically grown coffee won three prizes in 1999.

Some individuals and companies are making environmentalism a way of life. Youth for Environmental Sanity (YES) was founded in 1990 by 16-year-old Ocean Robbins (whose father walked away from the Baskin-Robbins ice cream empire and became a vegetarian activist) and his 19-year-old friend Ryan Eliason. With other inspired young people, they have gone on speaking tours to students in high school assemblies and college campuses, reaching over 610,000 people so far. YES has hosted summer training camps on 65 occasions, and inspired the creation of 400 clubs and non-profit organizations.

At the corporate level, Horizon Organic Dairy, headquartered in Boulder, Colorado, is building a new organic dairy on a 605-acre property in California. It arranged with the Nature Conservancy to make the land part of a preserve that is used by sandhill cranes, ducks, geese, and other migratory birds. Horizon will also restore a 110-acre freshwater marsh; use waste from the dairy farm as fertilizer; require suppliers to be organic, thus reducing fertilizer and pesticide runoff; and put straw and composting manure on the land. The cows receive organic feed but no antibiotics or growth hormones. Horizon is the country's leader in environmentally responsible dairy farming and in 2000 was given a Corporate Conscience Award by the Council on Economic Priorities. In 1997, *Inc.* magazine named it one of the country's fastest growing companies.

Throughout this book, you will see dozens more stories of environmental good news about people and institutions doing their share to help the earth. Visit our web site, *www.savenature.org/food* for more stories and send us yours!

PART I

Buying Your Food

OUR FOOD CHOICES, in sum, reverberate across the globe, determining how many endangered species and how many small-scale farmers will be driven off the land, how much rainforest will burn to keep our burgers cheap, and whether our grandchildren will ever know the taste of wild salmon.

—*Editors of Sierra Magazine*

Where to find earth-friendly foods

Every day it gets easier to find earth-friendly foods. They're in super-market chains, health food stores, farmers markets, and subscription farms. Take a reconnaissance trip through your local supermarket. You'll find organic food in the produce section, meatless options in the freezers, new products such as soy-based entrees or low-fat items, diverse products such as Japanese eggplant or amaranth, and green seals, labels verifying that a product is organic or otherwise eco-friendly.

Health food stores are excellent sources of earth-friendly food. National chains such as Whole Foods and Wild Oats have a greater range of healthy, organic, and alternative foods and other products than mainstream grocery chains. Small independent health food stores can also be found, where the tastes of the community are reflected. Some other options you may not be familiar with, including farmers markets and subscription farms, are described later.

What you can do:

✓ Make a shopping list before leaving home.

✓ At your usual supermarket, take a few extra minutes to look closely at the grocery shelves to see what's available. Look on higher and lower shelves than you usually do. Check out aisles you usually skip.

✓ Try out a natural food store, if you haven't already.

✓ Don't shop on an empty stomach. It makes you more likely to buy junk or impulse food.

✓ Ask yourself, "Will I really use this? When and how?"

Organic food

Modern agriculture drenches food in chemicals: pesticides to kill insects, herbicides to kill weeds in the fields, and antibiotics and hormones in cows, pigs, and chickens. Food that goes to a cannery or other processing plant gets additives and preservatives as well. It's estimated that each American eats 150 pounds of additives a year, including 130 pounds of sweeteners, 10 to15 pounds of salt, plus another 5 to10 pounds of flavorings, preservatives, and dyes. A single dose of pesticides may not be dangerous, but the impact accumulates over a lifetime. DDT was outlawed in 1972, but most people who were alive then still carry DDT residue such as DDE. It would be illegal to sell mothers' milk if it were packaged—it's too toxic. In 1999, 350 human-made pollutants were found in mothers' milk in England, some at concentrations 40 times the maximum recommended by World Health Organization.

- Over 12,000 chemicals and 3,000 additives are used to produce our food. As of 1995, there was toxicity information on only 54 percent of the food additives and a complete health risk assessment on only 5 percent.

- Seventy percent of the strawberries tested by the FDA in 1995 had chemical residues—of 30 different pesticides! The typical apple has had four different pesticides applied to it, and some have had as many as 10.

- The Consumers' Union, which produces *Consumer Reports*, found that 77 percent of conventionally grown produce samples had pesticide residues, while 25 percent of organic produce had some residues. The type of pesticide used also matters; the organic was far less toxic.

Growers may spray chemicals on a crop repeatedly through its growing season. For example, apple trees are sprayed once during winter dormancy, again when plants begin to bud, again after flowers are pollinated, and several more times while the apples are growing. The ripe fruit is sprayed with fumigants and waxes to make it look good. Sales of pesticides in the last 30 years have increased 27 times to a rate of $30 billion a year worldwide.

Methyl bromide, a highly toxic gas used to fumigate houses, commodities, and soil, is classified as an ozone-destroying chemical and is responsible for up to 10 percent of ozone depletion worldwide. Pesticides also kill pollinators (bees and birds that pollinate plants and make them fertile) and create secondary pests (creatures that were once innocuous but that multiply once we've killed their predators with pesticides). It costs $50 per acre per year in the United States to clean up after modern agriculture—removing pesticides from drinking water, repairing soil erosion, and dealing with air pollution and other messes. This doesn't include costs for damage to our health, the reduced effectiveness of antibiotics, or loss of diversity.

Laws may have banned certain chemicals, but American companies still produce them and export them to other nations that have less stringent laws. Industries fight new regulations and frequently manage to get a grace period before the laws take effect so that their existing stocks of chemicals can be sold. We import $37 billion of food from other countries a year ($4 billion in fresh fruits and vegetables), so the chemicals banned here may end up in your body anyway.

You can help your health, organic farmers, and the earth with one simple choice: buy more organic foods. There are 8,000 organic farms in the United States covering over 2 million acres.

What exactly is organic farming? There is no one definition, but it typically includes these features:

- Pests are controlled by crop rotation, cover crops, planting in small plots instead of huge ones, and introducing beneficial insects that eat the undesirable ones. If any chemicals are used, they are the least toxic ones.

- Organic land must be free of forbidden substances for three years before the organic label is granted; it must have a 25-foot buffer zone to protect it from the drift of chemicals used in neighboring fields; and farmers must keep detailed records of materials and substances used and allow annual inspections.

- No sewage sludge is used as fertilizer. Sewage sludge contains an unknown range of chemicals, toxins, and microbes.

- Specific rules must be followed for feeding, housing, and medically treating livestock, minimizing the use of antibiotics.

- No genetically engineered or irradiated food can be labeled organic.

- Specific regulations must be followed for chemicals, including cleansers and disinfectants, used in food processing plants that package organic foods.

Organic farming involves ingenuity, knowing one's land, and banding with other farmers to share ideas and market together. For example, the Food Alliance, a cooperative based in Portland, Oregon, helps small farmers publicize and market their goods and network with each other. Organic grapes are big business in California. After letting the land rest from years of pesticide use, growers thin the foliage so sun and wind kill mold and mildew, and then they spray vines with natural minerals (sulfur, lime, copper sulfate) that don't enter the vine's veins. They also plant blackberries on the borders, which lure good predator insects. It's even possible to buy organic coffee. Since coffee is grown in tropical regions where pesticides and herbicides damage many species, this is particularly important.

At present, organic farmers need to charge more because they are building their market, but prices are expected to go down as organic growing becomes more established. Almost half of organic sales are through conventional supermarkets; most of the rest is sold at natural food stores. Organic may be presently outside the budget for some people. To protect their health, they can wash conventional produce, as some experts recommend, and contribute to earth-friendly eating by making some of the other choices we suggest.

Goodbye to pesticides

Ending pesticide use can pay off. In Indonesia, rice fields were plagued by pesticide-resistant brown plant hoppers. In 1986, the government withdrew its $100 million pesticide subsidies, banned 57 pesticides, and created a national integrated pest management program. Since then, pesticide use has gone down by 60 percent, but rice harvests have increased by 25 percent.

The foods most important to buy organic

- ✓ Baby food
- ✓ Milk and butter
- ✓ Fruits: strawberries, bananas, peaches, cherries, nectarines, apricots, apples, grapes, melons, red raspberries, pears
- ✓ Vegetables: bell peppers, lettuces, spinach, green beans, tomatoes, cucumbers
- ✓ Protein foods: eggs, seafood, and meat
- ✓ Beverages: coffee, wine
- ✓ Foods containing soy and corn, to avoid genetically modified food.

What you can do

- ✓ Buy organic produce.
- ✓ Wash or peel nonorganic produce.
- ✓ Check labels.

Reducing antibiotics in animal feed: it works!

In Denmark, livestock growers reduced their annual antibiotic use by 75% between 1994 and 2000. As hoped, a bacterium that had become resistant to front-line antibiotics has declined. In more good news, there has been little increase in animal diseases that the antibiotics might have combated.

Green seals, green hats, and greenwash

How do you know which products are good for the earth and which are not? To help consumers identify green growers and manufacturers, various groups are certifying products and foods. "California certified organic" is a label that, in the absence of national standards, has been widely recognized. The "farmed free" seal was announced in September 2000 to indicate more humane treatment of animals. Farmers who win this seal must eliminate cages for laying hens and stop forced molting (starving hens of food and water, which paradoxically increases egg production). This is a step in the right direction. The non-profit Institute for Agriculture and Trade Policy is currently developing an international directory of label groups, label advocates, and related organizations. There are also voluntary initiatives like Greener Fields and the Food Alliance. The Consumers' Union web site (*www.eco-label.org*) explains and lists organic products.

The new USDA organic labels, applying to fruits, vegetables, and meat, will begin appearing in stores in 2002. "100 percent organic" means the product is made entirely of organically grown ingredients. "Organic" means it is made of at least 95 percent organic ingredients. "Made with organic ingredients" means at least 70 percent of the ingredients are organic. If less than 70 percent is made of organic ingredients, the food maker may list organic ingredients separately in the information panel. Start watching for these labels. Don't be surprised if they vary slightly from each other or if you read about disagreements between certifying organizations.

Even before national labels were established, some businesses were taking steps to be more earth-friendly—wearing "green hats." Ben and Jerry's ice cream pioneered business with a conscience, and others are following suit. Fetzer vineyards uses 100 percent renewable energy (solar, for instance), offers organic wine among its products, and aims to be 100 percent organic by 2010. The juice company Odwalla uses no preservatives, buys from farmers who are transitioning to organic, turns leftover fruit pulp into animal feed, is switching its fleet to natural gas-powered trucks, gives to Second Harvest, and sponsors interns at Earth College, an educational institution in Costa Rica. Snack maker FritoLay recovers 40 million pounds of potato starch from its wastewater and saves 400,000 gallons of heating oil by reusing heat from its cooking operations. New Organics, founded in 1997, markets 140 products in 3,600 grocery stores, including major chains. The company certifies 134 organic foods, snacks, cereals, sauces, and fresh produce. Stonyfield Farms, the fifth-largest yogurt maker in the United States, gives grants to dairy farmers to encourage sustainable agriculture, puts environmental messages on its yogurt lids, gives 10 percent of its profits to organic farmer associations, and plants trees to offset its carbon dioxide emissions. Eden Foods, Food from the Hood, Frontier Natural Products, Equal Exchange, and Newman's Own are other companies that sell organic products.

Beware of greenwash, however! This occurs when businesses try to seduce you with ads showing cute animals or packaging with green colors without making their product sustainable. Greenwash exists wherever dishonest producers deceive us, hide their real environmental impact, fight the prospect of regulation by claiming that they will start policing themselves, or create front organizations with earth-friendly names to mislead consumers. The EPA warns us about claims that are vague and meaningless, such as "eco-friendly" or "degradable." Look instead for specific claims—what percent of the content is recycled or organic? Greenpeace has developed a comprehensive checklist to help you assess a corporation's earth-friendliness. They abbreviate it as CARE:

- **Core business.** Is the company's core business basically destructive? It's not enough to produce a little solar energy if its major business is cutting down forests.
- **Advertising record.** There are 10 United States companies whose annual advertising budget is $1 billion or more. If the company's advertising emphasizes a few green products but the company mostly makes destructive ones, that's greenwash.
- **Research and development.** Is the company investing in sustainability?
- **Environmental lobbying.** If the company lobbies against environmental regulations and tries to defeat laws that would help the earth, or closes plants and exports jobs while claiming to be environmentally responsible, that's greenwash.

The Council on Economic Priorities studied and graded corporations for over 30 years, giving ratings on environment, gender and race equality, workplace issues, charitable giving, and other factors. Its 2000 report gave top grades to some food companies for their environmental record and very low grades to others (mostly meat producers).

What you can do

✓ Look for green labels.

✓ Don't be fooled by vague claims (i.e., "earth-friendly") or cuddly pictures and green colors on the labels.

✓ Tell your corner market that you want to buy soy milk and frozen vegeburgers. Let your local businesses know why you're shopping or dining there.

✓ Expect debates about what exactly constitutes organic. Realize that the concept is still unfolding.

Animal and land protectors in unexpected places

Zoos have become advocates for saving nature. The American Zoo Association (AZA), with 185 member zoos and aquariums, hosts conferences and sponsers research and land preservation in many countries. Member zoos do not accept animals taken from the wild and many of them conduct research and support conservation. For instance, the Oakland Zoo sends money to Uganda to sponsor environmental education and equip rangers so they can protect rain forest animals. It sends the Conservation Zoomobile to schools to teach children about rain forests, endangered species, and recycling. The Oakland Zoo works with the city to restore a creek on its land, sells shade-grown coffee in its restaurant, leads overseas eco-tours twice a year, and participates in research on chimpanzees, bees, giraffes, and elephants.

Support your local farmer

Our food marketplace is vast in numbers, dollars, and miles. At any time of year we can get oranges and bananas shipped from faraway states, even overseas. Season and distance have been eliminated as factors in our food choices. However, we pay a price for this endless cornucopia. Shipping foods vast distances uses fuel and refrigerant chemicals and increases the risks of importing pests and microorganisms when the food comes from other countries. In the homogenized market, we lose our sense of season and place. Small growers can't compete with national companies, and this is one reason family farms have been disappearing.

- In the United States, food travels an average of 1,300 miles to reach you.

- Between 1969 and 1999, over 800,000 farms vanished, taken over by large corporations.

Currently, 1 percent of farms (by number) grow half of the United States farm production. This means that a few decision-makers at agribusiness corporations like Philip Morris, Cargill, Pepsi, Coca-Cola, ConAgra, Nabisco, and Anheuser-Busch can dictate how your food is grown.

By contrast, small farmers in your region can choose to contribute to keeping the earth healthier. Smaller plots attract fewer pests and therefore need less pesticides than huge monoculture plantings do. There's less loss and waste because distances between field and customer are shorter and because knowledgeable consumers are willing to accept less-than-perfect-looking fruits and vegetables. This produce has required much less gasoline and refrigeration to transport. And don't forget about another endangered species—farmers! Organic and sustainable agricultures are lifesavers for some of them. The small farmers who buck the trend toward industrialization—especially if they want to avoid chemicals—benefit from the popularity of organic foods, subscription farms, and farmers markets. In return, some make extra contributions to their communities, offering workshops on gardening or nutrition, helping create gardens in housing projects and schools.

There are four ways to buy locally grown food

- Patronize farmers markets found in local malls or other public places, where the people who grow your food or small-scale middle men arrive in their own trucks and set up stalls. Purchasing fresh produce directly from growers is a pleasant change from supermarket shopping and allows you to support small local farms. There are almost 3,000 farmers markets nationwide.

- Roadside stands and pick-your-own opportunities exist in rural regions, some of them not far from populated areas.

- You could grow some food yourself.

- In community-supported agriculture (also called subscription farming), farmers plant a variety of crops to provide a continuous succession of ripe goods. Fresh organic food is delivered to your home or to a specified pick-up location each week. Some CSA farms also offer honey, eggs, and meat, or other rural products such as wool. Some provide produce to local restaurants, roadside stands, or farmers' markets. There are over 2,000 subscription farms in the United States, each serving hundreds of households.

CSA has many advantages. Growers get a fair return on their labor, local communities retain the buyers' food dollars, regional biodiversity is promoted, stewardship of the land is encouraged, and small business is supported. Communication and cooperation among farmers are encouraged. All in all, community supported agriculture is one of the most exciting developments we've discovered. It gives farmers a chance to regain control of their livelihoods, the farms a chance to recover from pesticides, and purchasers a chance to participate in the healthy growing of earth's bounty.

What you can do
- ✓ Subscribe to a CSA farm.
- ✓ Shop at a farmers market to get to know your local CSA.
- ✓ Ask about working shares in the farm, whereby you exchange several hours of work for a discount on your food.
- ✓ Apprenticeships and work exchanges let people experiment with the work of growing their own food.

The many miles of a fast food meal in Seattle.

1. The cow is moved from Texas range to a Colorado feedlot to be fattened.
2. Corn from Nebraska goes to the feedlot to feed the cow.
3. Water from the Oglalla aquifer (under large portions of Colorado, Kansas, Nebraska, and Texas) is used to water the cow.
4. The cow is slaughtered and the parts shipped to Seattle.
5. Milk from a dairy in Washington is turned into cheese.
6. Tomatoes and lettuce from California's Central Valley become garnish.
7. Wheat from Idaho becomes the hamburger bun.
8. Potatoes from Idaho become the fries.
9. Corn oil from Nebraska is used to fry the french fries.
10. Salt from Louisiana is added.
11. Florida tomatoes are shipped to Pittsburgh to make ketchup.
12. Ketchup is shipped to Ohio, where aluminum and plastic ketchup pouches are manufactured.
13. Ketchup is shipped from Ohio to Seattle.
14. The box for the fries is made from pulp from an Arkansas mill.
15. Bauxite from Australia is imported to make aluminum.
16. Calcium oxide from Japan is used to process the bauxite.
17. Aluminum can goes from smelter to canner.
18. Corn from Iowa becomes the corn syrup to sweeten the cola.

Saving the family farm

The Marin Agricultural Land Trust, the first of its kind in the nation, holds conservation easements protecting almost 30,000 acres from urban sprawl. This allows 43 family farms to stay in business. There are now more than 1,000 such trusts nationwide.

The truth about meat

The best food choice you can make for the earth is to eat less meat. Meat represents an inefficient use of the food supply because it takes seven to eight pounds of grain to produce one pound of beef. Meat also compromises our health, since pesticides and herbicides from growing all that grain get concentrated in the animals' bodies, ending up in ours. Pesticides mostly come to us through meats and other food from animals. Less than 10 percent of our pesticide exposure comes through produce. Furthermore, antibiotics are given to factory animals, sometimes even before there is a health problem, because their living conditions are so appalling that the animals are plagued with diseases. Growth hormones are given so they'll put on weight. Clearing land for cattle range and crops reduces the amount of vegetation, especially mature trees, available to take up greenhouse gases. Also, cows release methane, a greenhouse gas. These factors lead to air quality damage. Soil damage occurs because cattle cause soil erosion, compaction, and trampling of creeks. Chemicals and pesticides sprayed on the crops grown to feed cattle further damage the soil. The harm extends beyond these problems to include loss of diversity. Range land is cleared for cattle or otherwise degraded by them, destroying the habitats of prairie dogs, wolves, birds, deer, and other animals. Ranchers kill wild animals they believe threaten their herds. Finally, the runoff harms oceans, streams, and lakes. Chemicals used on land end up in the water, injuring or killing the fish and mammals that live there.

What are we eating?

- Six billion farm animals are killed for meat in the U.S. annually. Sixteen million animals are killed every day.

- Ninety-five percent of eggs and chickens are factory farmed (raised in confined spaces in huge sheds housing thousands of birds in crowded cages).

- In 1950, world meat production per capita was about 38 pounds per person. In 1998, it was 80 pounds, more than doubling in half a century. It went up 26 percent just in those last eight years. Part of this occurred because people in developing nations became prosperous enough to increase their meat consumption.

Converting grain into meat absorbs a lot of earth's resources. In 1900, 10 percent of the world's grain went to animals. By the late 1990s, that figure was 45 percent—but in the United States it was 60 percent. By one calculation, a given amount of grain could feed five times as many people if we ate it directly rather than cycling it through animals and turning it into meat. It takes seven to eight pounds of grain to produce an added pound of live weight in a cow in a feedlot, and almost four pounds to do the same in pigs—but only about half of that added live weight is edible. Sixty to seventy percent of world's fish catch goes to feed livestock. The poultry and hog industries are the world's largest users of fish meal. Add in the other costs of producing meat, and we end up with only 6 percent as much food as we would if we ate the grain directly.

Is meat harming the earth? Decide for yourself. Here is a quick overview. Sixty-four percent of U. S. agricultural land goes to grow livestock feed, and over half of U. S. water goes to livestock. Compared to pasta, beef creates 20 times the amount of the land-use alteration, 17 times the water pollution from waste, 5 times the toxic water pollution from chemicals, and 3 times the greenhouse gas emission.

Beef requires three times as much water per pound as milk and pork, and 50 times as much as eggs. In 1999, when Hurricane Floyd hit North Carolina (where 9 million hogs are raised), hundreds of the hog farm cesspools flooded, sending millions of gallons of hog sewage into floodwaters. Such spills damage rivers and estuaries, kill millions of fish, and could contaminate groundwater for 40 years. One mishap in June, 1995, spilled 25 million gallons of hog waste, fouling over 22 miles of rivers. Runoff of pesticides, fertilizers, and waste from farms and feedlots is the nation's largest source of water pollution.

Food animals produce 13 times the amount of waste produced by humans. Their waste contains oxygen-depleting substances—the organic matter in manure consumes oxygen as it decomposes—as well as ammonia and pathogens. Beef and dairy cows produce by far the most waste. Imagine living near a facility that breeds hundreds or thousands of animals in confined spaces—operations run by huge corporations headquartered far away. Massive fans blow air out of the sheds where hundreds of hogs live in crowded pens. The waste from hog sheds is kept in huge multi-acre cesspools; some of it is sprayed untreated on nearby fields. The air near these places is so bad that working or playing outside is intolerable and respiratory illnesses are aggravated.

Seventy percent of antibiotics made in the United States go to livestock because the animals are so crowded they're vulnerable to disease and infection. Salmonella is becoming resistant to antibiotics, spawning new superbugs that have begun to cause human fatalities. Antibiotics and other drugs are being found in waters around the nation. Luckily, agencies worldwide are beginning to clamp down on antibiotic use in agriculture.

When cattle move in to an area, other animals and plants suffer. Perennial native grasses are replaced by annuals such as wheatgrass; other non-native species such as cowbirds threaten local birds. Desert tortoises, cottonwood trees, and golden trout are just a few of the other species impacted. Mountain lions, bobcats, foxes, and other predators are legally killed by ranchers. Sedimentation and erosion occur when cattle graze in and around streams. Trampling causes erosion in creeks and slopes, ultimately harming floodplains.

Your tax dollars are involved. In 1999, a rancher paid $1.35 a month per steer to graze it on federal land. This is less than it costs to feed a house cat. Private grazing costs 10 times as much. Two hundred seventy million acres of American land are used for subsidized grazing—equal in size to California and Texas combined. The Green Scissors Coalition found that grazing fees recover only $25 million of the $77 million it costs to run the subsidy program.

Is it healthy to eat less (or no) meat?
In this country, we once believed that eating meat three times a day was a sign of worldly success. We believed that you risked your health if you didn't get a lot of protein from meat. In fact, the opposite may be true. The average man actually needs about 58 to 63 grams of protein a day, and the average woman 45 to 50 grams. (Obviously, such averages don't state what any given individual needs.) Protein comes in meat, dairy, and eggs—but also in nuts, beans, legumes, and some vegetables. Researchers have found that a person can be perfectly healthy with little or no meat. Though some people do not thrive on vegetarian diets, people who eat little or no

15

meat are often healthier than those who eat a lot. Cardiologist Dean Ornish has proved to a once-skeptical medical community that it is possible to reverse heart disease by a program of vegetarian food, exercise, yoga, and meditation.

Heavy meat consumption can stress your body. In one study, women over 65 who ate the most acidic diet (rich in meat and dairy) had 3.7 times more hip fractures than those with the least acidic diets. Eating high on the food chain exposes us to the pesticides from all the grain the cows ate and the toxins in the oceans the fish swam in. Most at risk for adverse effects due to pesticides, including the carcinogen dioxin, are people who eat a diet high in animal fat. At least one growth hormone given to U.S. cattle can cause cancer, immune problems, developmental problems, and brain disease. In fact, counting damage to people and the earth, "The most dangerous weapon in the arsenal of *Homo sapiens* is the table fork," says Howard Lyman, a former cattle rancher turned vegetarian activist.

What If . . .?

The cereal and grain eaten by the animals we raise for food could feed 3 billion people on a mostly vegetarian diet. According to fitness and health advocate Harvey Diamond, if Americans reduced their meat consumption by 10 percent, we could feed 60 million people on the saved grain. (10 percent is less than one meatless day a week.) We would also save annually: 1.5 trillion gallons of water, 500 billion gallons of manure which would not be produced, 2.3 billion gallons of fossil fuel, 12 million tons of grain, 700 million tons of soil, 128 million acres of land we could use for something else, 25 million acres of trees, and 600 million animals saved from slaughter.

What you can do

- ✓ Eat less meat. Have some meals with no meat, or one meatless day a week.
- ✓ Eat smaller portions. Stretch meat in soups and stews, using spices to make them interesting.
- ✓ Go vegetarian. Vegeburgers are delicious. Soy is nature's-perfect food.

✓ If you eat meat, buy organic and humanely raised meat. "Farmed free" meat is certified to be from humanely run farms. USDA organic meat will mean animals are raised more humanely and safely.

✓ Support farm sanctuaries, where cows, sheep, chickens, and other animals live out their lives in safety.

Don't Eat Your Fellow Actors

"I was so moved by the intelligence, sense of fun, and personalities of the animals I worked with on *Babe* that by the end of the film I was a vegetarian."

—*Actor James Cromwell*

Everybody wins

Straw from California rice fields was suspected of causing lung disease among citizens living downwind when growers burned the straw at the end of the season. To solve the problem, some growers flooded their fields after harvest instead, which created habitats for millions of migrating ducks and other wild birds. Other benefits followed: decomposing rice stubble rebuilt the soil and the ducks' favorite food animals—worms, arthropods, minnows—came to live in the seasonal wetlands. Hunters paid to visit the land. The natural fertilizers meant less artificial input was needed. Crop yields and net incomes rose. According to the authors of *Natural Capitalism*, "Now those farmers, with 30 percent of California's rice acreage, consider rice a coproduct of new businesses, providing water management, wildlife habitat, straw production, and other services."

Dairy

Dairy products seem so healthy and innocuous—almost mythically innocent and nourishing. But contrary to the claims of well-funded ad campaigns, milk is not so healthy after all. Milk, cheese, and other dairy products are linked to allergies, heart disease, and increased cholesterol. Ironically, milk even seems to weaken bones.

- In rural China, where cows' milk is not a big part of the diet, breast cancer deaths average 8.7 per 100,000 people. By contrast, the U.S. rate is 44 per 100,000—five times as high.

- Studying 6,500 rural families whose diet was nearly vegetarian, researchers found a similar difference in bone health. American women over age 50 had five times the hip fracture rate as the Chinese women.

- Of 78,000 nurses studied, those who drank the most milk had the most hip fractures.

- Over a ten-year period, 21,000 male doctors were studied. The milk drinkers had 30 percent more prostate cancer. In another study, milk-drinking men had 70 percent more prostate cancer.

- Pesticide levels in the milk of vegan mothers are only 1 to 2 percent of that of the general population. Put another way, a meat-eating mother has pesticide levels in her milk 50 to 100 times greater than that of a vegan (a vegetarian who does not eat dairy or eggs).

How can the facts be so different from what we've always been taught about cow's milk? That image of "nature's perfect food" came from ad campaigns paid for by the dairy industry. In the United States, the dairy industry is subsidized by the government. In turn, the dairy industry funds research and gives free educational materials to schools, where milk is required in school lunches. For most people, dairy isn't dangerous in reasonable quantities. (However, some people, such as African Americans and Asians, have lactose intolerance in greater proportions than Caucasians do.) Quantity is what matters in the long run. The studies suggest that the less dairy a population consumes, the healthier it is.

"Every 30 seconds on this continent, Canada included, somebody grabs their chest and falls over with a heart attack. This is animal fat clogging up the arteries. When you send this material down to the pathologist and you ask him to analyze it, the report always comes back the same. Saturated fat and cholesterol. It's animal fat. The pathology report never, ever, ever contains the words: remnants of broccoli, rice, and tofu."

—*Michael Klaper, MD*

Dairy isn't good for earth, either. Many of the problems associated with beef cattle apply to dairy cattle. In addition, water used to irrigate pastures could meet the domestic needs of 22 million people. Each dairy cow produces up to 22 tons of waste a year. Sixteen hundred dairies in California's Central Valley produce more waste than a city of 21 million. Such waste even pollutes the air.

You do need calcium. It's available in vegetables such as collard greens and broccoli, and in fruits such as figs. One expert who participated in the China study said, "Quite simply, the more you substitute plant foods for animal foods, the healthier you are likely to be." A study at Harvard University concluded, "Traditional diets associated with good health and lengthy adult life expectations are generally plant-based—rich in whole grains, vegetables, fruits, and nuts—supplemented by sparing amounts of animal products."

The American Cancer Society states that a good diet should limit consumption of meats, especially high-fat meats, and emphasize beans, grains, and vegetables. The American Dietetic Association announced a few years ago that "it is the position of the American Dietetic Association (ADA) that appropriately planned vegetarian diets are healthful, are nutritionally adequate, and provide health benefits in the prevention and treatment of certain diseases." Finally, the Physicians' Committee for Responsible Medicine says unequivocally, "Vegan diets are the healthiest of all."

What you can do

✓ Reduce the amount of dairy you consume.

✓ Experiment with tofu, soy milk, and almond and rice drinks.

✓ Try using less cheese in your cooking.

✓ If you use dairy, buy organic or farmed free products.

Fish

We may think there are literally oceans of fish living in natural habitats, reproducing freely, as inexhaustible as the seas. Sadly, this is not true. We threaten fish (and crustaceans, mollusks, and marine mammals) by overfishing and polluting their world.

Overfishing

Though overfishing is not new, modern methods take this to an extreme. Vast fleets of floating packing factories armed with sonar and advanced technologies are so efficient that their activities have been called "underwater clear-cutting" and "underwater strip-mining." Overfishing depletes fish populations and robs other marine animals of food, endangering biodiversity and whole ocean communities. Fishing methods include metal chain dredges that pull up boulders and uproot living organisms that attach to seafloors. Nets with rubber tires attached allow fishers to troll over rocky bottoms that were once inaccessible. Seventy percent of the world's fish populations are overfished, according to a study sponsored by the United Nations and the World Bank. The oceans are being emptied up to 150 times faster than forests are being cleared.

Jobs disappear when fisheries go out of business from overfishing; 40,000 jobs were lost when Canada's Atlantic cod fishery collapsed in the 1990s.

Bycatch and competition

Even species that are not wanted for food are at risk. In 1990, 42 million marine mammals (such as dolphins and sea lions) were caught by drift nets. In Japan, porpoises are herded into bays and slaughtered because they compete with humans for fish. For every pound of shrimp caught, seven pounds of other sea life are killed.

Science teacher Andrew Snow served as a biological observer for five years, living and working on Russian, Korean, and Japanese trawlers to enforce fishing regulations in the 200-mile economic zone around the United States. Each trawler put out a dragnet half a mile wide at the mouth and 100 yards wide at the narrow end, 3 to 5 times a day for 4 to 5 hours each time, and dragged it across the ocean floor, scraping off all life in its path. One ship could catch 500 tons, but it also brought up crabs, shellfish, sea stars, and mammals. The crews left the unwanted animals to die on the deck or in the hold, and dumped them overboard before the catch was weighed. Some boats would seek out breeding grounds, catching 300 to 400 tons of fish a day. Since freezer space was valuable, they kept only the eggs and threw the fish overboard. Corals were carelessly destroyed if they got in the way; five-foot-high, beautiful cone-shaped sponges were torn off, crushed, and thrown overboard. Snow estimates that a fleet of six trawlers threw out 100,000 tons of sea life in one six-week season. He also saw American trawler workers shoot sea lions and killer whales that were attracted by nets full of fish.

Dead zones and dams

Agricultural runoff enters creeks and flows downstream to lakes and oceans. Excess nutrients from fertilizers, especially phosphorus and nitrogen, are killing marine life in more than a third of our coastal areas. Scientists calculate that nitrogen runoff has tripled and phosphorus runoff has doubled in the last 40 years, leading to bioaccumulation. They found severe problems in 44 of 139 coastal areas studied. Fish swimming in the pools of our toxins can absorb pesticides, dioxins, PCBs, cadmium, and mercury, dangerous substances that end up in our food supply. Oceans are beginning to resemble open sewers. There are at least 50 dead zones in the oceans. The largest is in the Gulf of Mexico where the Mississippi River empties into it. This dead zone is now larger than the state of New Jersey and has doubled in size since 1993.

MUTTS   **BY PATRICK M^cDONNELL**

Mutts cartoons reprinted with special permission of King Feature Syndicate

Another kind of danger for fish is created by our dams. To provide reservoirs and cheap energy, we have dammed the nation's rivers. Salmon in the Pacific Northwest find it almost impossible to reach their home streams to breed and produce the next generation.

Safer, saner fishing

For years, some fishers in tropical seas have used destructive methods that dragged up huge chunks of coral reef or even used cyanide and dynamite to kill some fish and make others float to the surface. An invention is helping stop these practices. Fish aggregating devices (FADs) are anchored devices that attract fish and lure fishers away from reefs.

Human health

Besides agricultural and industrial runoff, other sources of water pollution exist, such as ship fuel and raw waste discharged into the water. Burning fossil fuels release mercury into the air, which ultimately enters oceans. We have polluted the rivers and oceans so much that the fish living in them are a danger to us.

- Every year, 60,000 babies are born in the United States with neurological problems caused by mercury—some of it from fish.

- Whales caught by Norwegians have so much toxic PCBs in their blubber (over seven times Japan's maximum permitted level) that Japanese consumer groups warn against eating what is to them a delicacy.

- In California, gold miners in the 1850s used millions of pounds of mercury in their hydraulic mining operations. Fish living in waters nearby still have dangerous mercury levels and have been declared unsafe for human consumption. What humans did 150 years ago is impacting us today.

Fish farming

Fish farming, also known as aquaculture, would seem like the answer. Operators build large pens where they grow thousands of salmon, shrimp, and other fish. However, like other animals raised in huge numbers in confined places, farmed fish are susceptible to disease and are given antibiotics, which also enter the waterways. Some, like salmon and shrimp, are carnivorous, and must be fed other fish—which come from the oceans. One expert calculated that it takes two to three pounds of wild-caught fish to raise one pound of salmon or shrimp; another expert thinks the ratio is closer to five to one. Large tracts of the world's coastal forests and wetlands have been destroyed by coastal development or shrimp pond aquaculture. As with cattle, antibiotics and pesticide runoff lead to diseases, resistant bacteria, and loss of genetic diversity among fish. When hatchery fish escape or are released, they outcompete and deplete wild fish populations.

National laws and international treaties protect a few species, such as whales and dolphins. But the treaties have been watered down, poorly enforced, or even repealed. For instance, Japan catches whales for scientific research of dubious value and sends their flesh to meat-packing plants. Government agencies ignore, selectively enforce, or actively violate laws. Sanctuaries are not guarded or actually permit fishing, boating, or mining. Pirate ships and "flag of convenience" ships ignore treaties. There's one bit of good news. At the end of 2000, a U.S. law was enacted banning the practice of catching sharks, cutting off their fins (a delicacy in Asia), and throwing the mutilated shark back in the ocean to die a slow death. Let's hope more such laws are passed—and enforced.

What you can do:

✓ Eat less seafood or none at all.

✓ Choose the less endangered species.

✓ Encourage aquaculture if it is operated sustainably, producing fish low on the food chain such as tilapia, carp, milkfish, or mullet.

✓ Because of endangered status, contamination, or both, do not eat swordfish, abalone, orange roughy, grouper, Atlantic cod, haddock, yellowtail tuna, flounder, monkfish, scallops, Chilean sea bass, shark, shrimp, farmed salmon, American lobster, bluefin tuna, lingcod, rockfish, Pacific red snapper, or rock cod.

✓ Fish facts are volatile, so keep up to date. See these sites:
  -Audubon Society: *www.audubon.org/campaign/lo*
  -Chef's Collaborative: *www.chefnet.com/cc2000*
  -Environmental Defense Fund: *www.environmental/defense.org*
  -Monterey Bay Aquarium: *www.montereybayaquarium.org*
  -Marine Stewardship Council: *www.msc.org*
  -National Resources Defense Council: *www.nrdc.org/wildlife/fish*

✓ Use less energy in all of your activities to reduce the perceived need for hydroelectric dams.

Setting limits on themselves

A new system involves sharing power between the fishing industry and government agencies. A 1995 law allowed lobster fishers in Maine to help manage zones, in elected councils in which license holders propose rules (the number of traps each license holder may set, times of day, and so on). By 1998, all zones had voted for trap limits well below what state law allowed.

Soy, plant proteins, and vegeburgers

Soybeans are low on the food chain and full of protein. Soy can be turned into a dazzling array of things, from soy milk to tofu, baked goods, vegeburgers, and more. Soy not only avoids the health problems associated with cows' milk, it offers positive health benefits of its own. Soy helps reduce cancer and heart disease, lowers heart disease risk by lowering cholesterol, helps prevent osteoporosis, diabetes, kidney trouble, and cancer, and eases the symptoms of menopause. Chain grocery stores and natural food stores stock soy products in amazing variety.

The burger is the quintessential American meal. Fortunately, there's a way to have one and be kind to the earth. Vegeburgers come in many delicious flavors and are made of oats, grains, beans, and chopped vegetables; some include tofu or cheese. You can buy them at your regular grocery store or at a natural grocery. Many restaurants now offer vegeburgers, so you can continue to patronize your favorite establishments. The market for vegeburgers alone was almost $350 million in 2000.

- A vegetarian eats about 2,500 calories a day from crops; a meat eater consumes 9,000 calories' worth, much of it cycled through animals.

- It takes at least 45,000 square feet of land to feed a person on a high-meat diet, but only 10,000 square feet to feed a vegetarian.

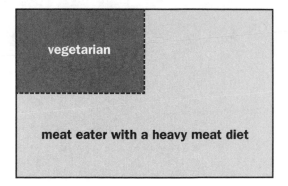

vegetarian

meat eater with a heavy meat diet

What you can do:

- ✓ Buy the soybeans themselves, which cook like any other legume.

- ✓ Drink soy milk hot, serve it cold with cereals, and use it in recipes that call for milk.

- ✓ Use tofu as you would use eggs in a wide variety of baked goods, scrambles, marinades, casseroles, and more.

- ✓ Try tempeh (a fermented form of soy), miso (a bouillon-like concentrate for soups), and frozen tofutti desserts.

- ✓ Try vegeburgers, tofuburgers, and tempehburgers—prepared patties of various consistencies and flavorings.

Mad Cowboy is astonished

The Mad Cowboy, as ex-cattle-rancher Howard Lyman calls himself, became a vegetarian activist, criss-crossed the nation on speaking tours, and finally wrote a book. He says: "While writing my book I returned to Montana. At the largest commercial supermarket in Great Falls, I could hardly believe my eyes. Soy milk and rice milk on the shelves. Soy hot dogs, veggie burgers, tofu, seitan. It's not hard any more to be a vegetarian in America. If it can be done in Great Falls, it can be done anywhere."

Fruits, vegetables, and grains

Recall that seven crops account for 75 percent of our food. Such over-specialization leads to problems. For example, modern corn, which is used in almost 200 food products, clothing, drugs, and cosmetics, was decimated by a fungus in 1970. Fortunately, there were still some wild varieties in existence; genetic material from the wild helped breed resistance to the fungus into the corn crop. However, we are ignoring even these proven benefits of diversity. Nearly 96 percent of the commercial vegetable varieties available in 1903 are extinct.

Monoculture, planting huge fields of a single variety, is not the most productive system. Proof of this came in a study whose results were announced in mid-2000. Tens of thousands of Chinese farmers were instructed not to plant large stands of one kind of rice, but to alternate smaller plots of two kinds of rice. The results were stunning. With only this one change, rice yields doubled. Experts are convinced that this will work with other crops.

Currently, farm subsidies go to the biggest farms and encourage agribusiness operators to grow the same amounts of the same crops every year. This discourages crop rotation and encourages pesticide and fertilizer use. Furthermore, seed companies are being bought by agrochemical corporations; 1,000 independent seed companies have been bought by transnational chemical and pharmaceutical companies in the last 20 years. Ironically, the plant extinctions we are witnessing actually harm pharmaceutical interests. The EPA commented, "The lost pharmaceutical value from plant extinctions in the United States alone is almost $12 billion."

Fortunately, individuals and groups like Seed Savers have rescued many varieties, keeping genetic material alive. To encourage farmers to grow a wider range of fruits, grains, and vegetables, we must give them a market. You could buy unusual varieties of familiar foods such as apples and potatoes, buy unusual foods, or even grow some unusual varieties in your garden.

There are 2,500 apple varieties grown in the United States, though only about 100 varieties are commercially grown. Fifteen of these (such as Red Delicious) account for about 90 percent of the total U.S. apple production. Look for Pink Ladies, Cameos, Criterions, Jonagolds, and other varieties. Potato varieties also exist: Yukon Gold, and other gour-

27

met potatoes are now trendy. Kennebec, Norchip, Norkotah, Shepody, Sebago, and other varieties may be found in local farmers markets. Tomatoes come with the wonderful names of Sun Gold, Brandywine, Dona, Black Prince, Stupice, Isis Candy, Green Zebra, Earl of Edgecombe, and Costoluto Genovese.

Besides the apples and pears we're familiar with, it is becoming easier to find exotic fruits and vegetables: carambola, cherimoya, atemoya, feijoa, guava, purple passionfruit, persimmon, and tamarillo. Remember when kiwis were exotic? In addition, grains such as amaranth, kamut, spelt (also called farro), and quinoa (pronounced keenwa) are finding a place in American cuisine. Ethnic cuisines are sources of ideas about diversity—eggs from quail and duck or other birds, unusual fish, and organ meats. In some cultures, it's common to eat insects—fried ants in Mexico, termite and palm grubs in Colombia, grasshoppers and crickets in the Philippines. That's really eating low on the food chain!

You can encourage biodiversity by broadening your range of fruits and vegetables. It's easier than ever. Between 1987 and 1997, the number of items in supermarket produce departments almost doubled. Experiment with foods you've never tried. Wander down the international section of your grocery store. Linger at the farmers market to see what's there. Shop in a part of town you don't usually visit. You might find such fruits and vegetables as banana blossoms, durian, lotus roots, suiqua, rau den, wal quay sum, gai lan, gai choy, nagaimo, and seaweed from Chinese markets. From Mexico we get a variety of red corn, tomatillos, and nopales (cactus). The Hmong people from Southeast Asia eat lemongrass, red basil, bitter eggplant, and lotus roots. Your region may have other intriguing ethnic cuisines.

BC cartoon by permission of Johnny Hart and Creators Syndicate, Inc.

28

Where to find unusual foods:

- ✓ Your regular supermarket produce department, which may have greater choice than you ever noticed. Be sure to check out the ethnic aisles.
- ✓ Natural grocery stores such as Wild Oats and Whole Foods.
- ✓ Farmers markets.
- ✓ Community supported agriculture.
- ✓ Ethnic food stores.

How to prepare them:

- ✓ Some grocery stores give out recipe sheets for unusual foods.
- ✓ Some fresh produce comes with stickers that give brief instructions (boil, ripe when soft, etc.).
- ✓ Canned goods may have cooking suggestions printed on the label.
- ✓ Search the Web for recipes—many sites offer recipes and food information.
- ✓ Explore the cookbook section of your local bookstore.

Diversity in sweeteners

Refined cane sugar is by no means the only ingredient we can use to sweeten food. Of course, we could always decide to use less. Americans consume an average of 20 teaspoons of added sugars a day, accounting for 16 percent of their calories. A can of soda contains the equivalent of 10 teaspoons of sugar. Six thousand kilocalories of energy are expended to produce enough beet sugar to supply only 3,800 kilocalories to the consumer. But, artificial sweeteners contribute to the total chemical load in our bodies.

So what could you use instead? You already know about honey. You could try different varieties, or look for brands that are organic. (Be sure not to give honey to infants, as it can be dangerous for them.) Other delicious alternatives include barley malt, molasses, fruit concentrate, beet sugar, and stevia (available at health food stores).

Coffee, tea, and other beverages

Beverages condense many of the issues we have been talking about: growing methods, packaging, and transport. Carbonated water may come from a natural source, but it involves packaging and trucking. Fruit juice may come from fruit grown with chemicals in huge monocultures and transported long distances. Regional franchises bottle the national brands of sodas, so there is less of a transportation problem, but aluminum cans are made of ore extracted at great cost, and we don't recycle all of them. The United States still gets about 60 percent of its aluminum from virgin ore, at 20 times the energy needed to recycle aluminum. We throw away enough aluminum to replace our entire commercial aircraft fleet every three months. Sodas have no nutritional value and many of them have caffeine and artificial dyes and sweeteners. Coffee is non-nutritive, grown far away, processed chemically, and full of caffeine, an addictive chemical.

Let's look more closely at coffee. The average U.S. coffee drinker consumes three cups a day, which over a year adds up to 50 gallons made from 27 pounds of beans, representing the production of 20 to 30 coffee plants. Growers apply 11 pounds of fertilizer and a few ounces of pesticide to the plants for this person. After harvest and processing, 43 pounds of coffee pulp go into local rivers, where it decomposes, taking up oxygen that fish need. Diesel-powered bean crushers are used to process the beans, and freighters using petroleum fuel bring them to the United States, where the roasting process burns natural gas. The final product is packaged in four-layer bags made of polyethylene, nylon, aluminum, and polyester.

In the modern sun growing method, trees are cut down to clear land. Biologists in Mexico found that traditional shade coffee plantations supported 180 species of birds but that 90 percent fewer bird species can live in sun fields. In the absence of birds, insects multiply, so more pesticides are used, as well as fertilizers. Sun coffee fields thus contribute to species loss, land erosion, water pollution, and health risks to workers.

Fortunately, organic coffee is a small but growing niche. The coffee is planted among the trees in the forest and not in cleared fields worked by machines. Merchants of Green Coffee require that the tree canopy must be 40 percent, native species must be present, no chemicals or plastic can be used, and the pulp must be composted. Coffee grown wisely is finding an appreciative audience. One third of America's consumption consists of specialty coffees sold at higher prices if they taste better or are grown under socially or environmentally responsible conditions. They are labeled "gourmet," "organic," "eco-friendly," and "fair traded." The case of coffee shows how consumer choices in one corner of the globe impact working conditions and the environment in another.

Harvest for Haiti, a California-based nonprofit, has partnered with three coffee cooperatives to assist in coffee development and marketing, keeping local farmers involved throughout the entire marketing and distribution process. This gives them a fairer share of the profit than they usually get when there are layers of middlemen. How does this help the environment? In Haiti's current economy, some impoverished farmers can make more money by cutting down fruit-bearing trees to sell as charcoal than they can by cultivating and selling their fruit. Harvest for Haiti's fair-trade coffee gives local farmers an alternative, which helps them and helps the earth.

What you can do:

✓ Buy organic, fairly traded, and shade-grown coffee.

✓ Use unbleached coffee filters.

✓ Try locally grown herbal tea.

✓ Buy in bulk.

✓ Reuse and then recycle the container.

✓ Try soy and almond drinks.

✓ Try diverse fruit juices.

✓ Encourage small regional juice makers, not just national brands.

✓ Make a quart of your favorite tea and keep it chilled in your fridge.

Packaging

A shocking amount of earth's resources goes into boxing, bottling, and canning the food that comes to you. Packaging uses 50 percent of all paper produced in the U.S., 90 percent of the glass, and 11 percent of the aluminum. Pulp and paper production is the world's fifth largest industrial user of energy. It also uses water and bleach and contributes significantly to air pollution. Food packaging accounts for 6 percent of U.S. energy consumption. Each U.S. citizen uses 730 pounds of paper and cardboard a year. The world average is 110 pounds; in developing nations, the average is 40.

A lot of packaging exists not to contain the food but to attract our attention with fancy boxes and colors. In 1998, $30 billion was spent to advertise food in the United States. Kellogg's spends $40 million a year just to advertise Frosted Flakes. Furthermore, packaging costs you immediately. If a family of four buys 45 gallons of orange juice a year (each person drinks half a cup a day), they can save $160 a year by buying in gallon instead of pint containers. The energy this saves just in manufacturing the containers could power a hall nightlight for 16 months. The University of Florida Extension Service, which discovered this, also estimated that:

- In 1984, the United States discarded 59.6 billion pounds of paper packaging. This represents 660 million trees and 17 billion gallons of gas to process and transport the packaging. (17 billion gallons of gas could keep a 60-watt light bulb burning for over 400 million years.)

- In 1987, 4.4 billion pounds of plastic film wrap were discarded. To produce this requires the equivalent of 2.8 billion gallons of gasoline (which could run a 20-cubic foot fridge for over 5 million years).

- If we reduced our plastic and paper packaging by only 10 percent, 6.4 billion pounds would be removed from the waste stream and the energy equivalent of 2 billion gallons of gas would be conserved. (Two billion gallons of gas would operate your television for 170 billion hours, which is 650 million years.)

Fortunately, some manufacturers are paying attention to this problem. Anheuser-Busch saves $250 million a year in materials by applying environmental initiatives in their packaging operations. Tom's of Maine, which makes toothpaste and other personal care products, is committed to operating on environmentally sound principles. They use no artificial or animal ingredients, renewable energy in their operations, recyclable packaging, organic ingredients, and expect their suppliers to be environmentally conscious, too. Tom's recently announced a five-year initiative, the "National Rivers Awareness Program," in partnership with The Nature Conservancy, the National Park Service, the River Network, and retailers. The goal is education and grassroots action (such as local cleanups) to restore the nation's rivers.

A family of four can save $3,000 a year by purchasing products in large sizes or reusable products: gallons of juice instead of individually packaged servings, large boxes of cereal instead of small ones, rechargeable batteries, cloth napkins and dish cloths instead of paper towels.

What you can do:

✓ Buy products with the least packaging.

✓ Buy products in large quantities, not tiny serving sizes.

✓ Consider using concentrates (juices, cleansers) that require less packaging.

✓ When buying a few small items, ask the clerk not to put them in a bag.

✓ Reuse and recycle the packaging you buy.

✓ Bring your own cloth bags or the paper bags from your las shopping trip.

Plastic for lunch

One year Florida had 165,375 students in the first grade. If they all used reusable plastic sandwich boxes instead of baggies, it would save the energy equivalent of over 125,000 gallons of gas a year. This is one kind of packaging for one state's children, in one grade, for one meal, for one school year.

Frozen, canned, and processed food

The environmental impact of any food—say, a green bean—depends partly on how it gets to your table. You have five choices.

- Growing your own food has the least impact on the environment. You can purchase a pound of green bean seeds and invest your time for weeding, watering, pest control, and perhaps using some fertilizer.

- If your green beans come from a local farmers market or produce stand, they have traveled far less than the average food, which travels 1,300 miles to your table. They might come from small-scale growers who have chosen earth-friendly farming practices.

- You can purchase your green beans from a supermarket produce department, probably the product of large-scale agriculture, which uses pesticides, herbicides, fertilizers, and long-distance transportation.

- You can purchase them canned or frozen, grown by large-scale agriculture. This includes all the environmental costs associated with supermarket produce, plus materials and energy used in canning or freezing.

- You can have them as a side dish in a frozen dinner entree. This includes all the costs associated with canned or frozen produce, plus more non-recyclable packaging and more additives, since the vegetables are fully cooked for inclusion in a frozen dinner.

Agribusiness grows most of its products for processing rather than for the fresh vegetable market; it's more profitable. Eighty percent of snap bean production in 1994 was grown for processing. We spend over $5 billion annually on frozen dinners and entrees. However, processing involves equipment to wash, sort, cook, and package the food. It displaces workers, since one mechanical harvester can replace as many as 100 manual pickers and their supervisors. This minimizes harvesting costs, but there is some reduction in quality. Then there is the environmental cost of building the machines (steel, plastic, etc.), the cost of the pollution generated by the operation of the machine, and the loss of employment for many of our nation's neediest residents.

The packaging itself is manufactured. More energy is expended to freeze the vegetable and transport it in a freezer rather than a cooled truck. Finally, processing usually robs foods of many of their natural nutrients, though processors often add these or other nutrients back in.

In large agribusiness, beans are almost always harvested by machines. Mechanical harvesters generally have opposing brushes that strip the pods from the vines, leaving only the plant stems. The harvested material is transported through various separators to remove dirt, leaves, and other foreign materials. The pods are then placed in bags, pallet bins, or dump hoppers for transport to the packing shed. Most of these machines have no means of discriminating between quality levels and will harvest immature, overmature, diseased, or damaged pods that would ordinarily be discarded by a human picker. Then more machines are needed to sort the pods.

French fries in fast food restaurants are probably Russet Burbanks. Ninety percent of Idaho's potatoes are of this variety because McDonald's and other fast food establishments prefer it. This reduces potato diversity. Seven and a half gallons of water are used to grow each potato. Most of the fields are irrigated with water diverted from rivers. This deprives fish of their habitat. Fertilizers and pesticides are used to grow the potato. In many agricultural communities that grow potatoes, groundwater supplies are contaminated with the runoff. The potato is harvested by a diesel machine and trucked to a processing plant. Processing it creates two thirds of a gallon of wastewater, which is sent back into the water table.

When the potatoes reach the factory, after conveyor belt sorting, they are steamed, shot through a water gun knife, and emerge as potato slices. Video cameras pick out imperfect ones, which are sent to separate machines that cut out flaws and return them to the line. They then move through more hot water, air, and oil to become fries. Air cooling by ammonia gas freezes them, and more machines sort, seal, and load them for shipping.

Freezing the potatoes requires electrical energy, encouraging the building of more hydroelectric dams, which continue to impact our waterways. The freezing process uses hydrofluorocarbon coolants. These are better than the older coolants, but they are still greenhouse gases. The distribution path includes a journey in a refrigerated 18-wheeler diesel truck. Finally, your fries are served in a cardboard carton, often with a handful of plastic ketchup packets. Many of these packets are discarded unopened into the trash bin.

What about packaged meals and entrees? Their ingredients move around from state to state, processing plant to processing plant to packaging plant, in what *New York Times* food writer Michael Pollan calls "an elaborate and energy-intensive choreography of ingredients."

What you can do:

✓ Buy more fresh produce.

✓ Buy locally grown produce.

✓ Buy products with the least processing and packaging.

Vegetable-based wrapping

There's hope for replacing plastic wrap. A USDA employee has invented a wrap made from fruits and vegetables. It looks like a sheet of paper and can be made of any fruit or vegetable. The wrap made of broccoli is tinted green; strawberries make a red wrap. The inventor is looking for a manufacturer to make this wrap commercially available. Corn is the basis for another plastic substitute.

Coffee and conservation

In Uganda, a project funded by the World Bank brings together the Uganda Wildlife Authority, Kibale National Park, Makerere University, Uganda Coffee Trade Federation, and local communities. Coffee grows wild near the national park, and the agreement allows local residents to harvest certified wild and organic coffee sustainably. The university's scientists monitor the growers, and local jobs are created. Profits go to parks and communities for conservation.

Number of steps for various processes

Home Grown	Community supported	Supermarket Fresh	Supermarket Processed	Frozen TV Dinner
Planting	Planting	Planting	Planting	Planting
Fertilizing	Fertilizing	Fertilizing	Fertilizing	Fertilizing
Watering	Watering	Watering	Watering	Watering
Protecting	Protecting	Protecting	Protecting	Protecting
Picking	Picking	Picking	Picking	Picking
	Sorting	Offloading belt	Offloading belt	Offloading belt
	Washing	Gravity	Gravity	Gravity
	Grading	separator	separator	separator
	Boxing	Trash	Trash	Trash
	Shipping	eliminator	eliminator	eliminator
		Pin-bean eliminator	Pin-bean eliminator	Pin-bean eliminator
		Broken-bean eliminator	Broken-bean eliminator	Broken-bean eliminator
		Vibrating tables	Vibrating tables	Vibrating tables
		Vibrating washers	Vibrating washers	Vibrating washers
		Grading tables	Grading tables	Grading tables
		Carousel-type automatic box filler	Carousel-type automatic box filler	Carousel-type automatic box filler
		Cooling	Cooling	Cooling
		Ship to Distribution center	Ship to processing plant	Ship to processing plant
		Ship to processing plant	Offloading belt	Offloading belt
		Ship to local store	Washing	Washing
			Cutting, trimming	Cutting, trimming
			Cooking with additives	Cooking with additives
			Inspecting	Inspecting
			Packaging	Adding to other foods
			Ship to Distribution Center	Double Packaging
			Ship to local store	Ship to Distribution Center
				Ship to local store

PART II

Meals at Home

THE VERY EATING HABITS that can do so much to give you strength and health are exactly the same ones that can significantly reduce the needless suffering in the world and do much to preserve our ecosystem. And you'll discover the profound liberation that comes from bringing your eating habits into harmony with life's deepest ecological basis.

—*John Robbins*

Use energy skillfully

You impact the earth by your choice of cooking methods and tools in the kitchen. The refrigerator is the biggest single user of household energy and impacts the environment in other ways. Hydrofluorocarbons (HFCs), the chemicals that cool refrigerators, are greenhouse gases, trapping the sun's heat and contributing to global warming. Meanwhile, generating the electricity to power the fridge emits carbon dioxide. So buying the most energy-efficient fridge is one of the smartest moves you can make. The modern kitchen is also filled with coffeemakers, grinders, blenders, microwave ovens, and more. Sometimes we use them wastefully—heating a large oven to warm a single muffin, using a special gadget to heat hot dogs, and cooking an eight-pound roast for hours.

Energy-efficient appliances and microwave ovens can help. A microwave oven uses only a third of the power of a full-sized oven and gives less heat to the kitchen. In summer, this reduces the temptation to turn on the air conditioning. A microwave cooks up to 75 percent faster and requires fewer cleanups since you can cook and serve in the same dish. This uses less hot water and soap.

Refrigeration

✓ Don't buy a bigger refrigerator than you need.

✓ Buy an energy-efficient one, preferably from a manufacturer that will take back your fridge when you are done with it in order to recover the coolant and other materials. "Take-back" marketing is common in Europe and should catch on in the United States.

✓ Fill the fridge less than three-quarters full to allow cool air to circulate. Check the door seals for leaks. Replace the gasket (the rubber seal around the door) if necessary.

✓ Brush or vacuum the dust and lint from the refrigerator coils, so the refrigerator cools more efficiently.

✓ Set the temperature at 38 to 42 degrees F, and the freezer at 0 to 5 degrees F.

✓ Cover foods and liquids, which keeps food from drying out and keeps the fridge from having to work to remove moisture.

✓ Let hot food cool on the counter before putting it in the fridge or freezer.

Oven

✓ If you're in the market for a new oven, consider buying a convection oven. It has a fan that distributes the heat evenly and speeds the cooking process.

✓ Don't preheat the oven unless the food requires a high temperature and a short (or precisely measured) cooking time.

✓ Devise all-oven meals—for instance, meat loaf, baked potatoes, and baked apples.

✓ Use glass and ceramic pans, which retain heat better than metal pans so that you can reduce the baking temperature by 25 degrees F.

✓ Don't put foil over the oven floor or racks, which alters the heat distribution.

✓ Use the smallest oven (or a toaster oven) you have for each task.

✓ Don't peek so often. The temperature drops each time the oven door is opened.

✓ After you are done cooking, use the leftover heat to warm up rolls or dessert, to dry dishes, or (in winter) to heat the kitchen.

Stovetop

✓ Cover pots while cooking. This simple step can reduce energy use by two thirds.

✓ Electric burners can be turned off a few minutes before the end of the scheduled cooking time. The unit is still hot and continues cooking the food.

✓ Clean the reflector pans under the stovetop heating elements so that heat reflects back to the pan.

✓ Use a pan the same size or a little bigger than the heating unit. If the pan is too large or too small, a lot of heat is wasted.

✓ Woks are good for cooking combinations of chopped vegetables.

✓ Electric kettles and microwaves are efficient for heating small amounts of water.

✓ Chinese steamers (stacks of permeable baskets) can cook several vegetables simultaneously on several levels.

Dishwasher

✓ Run the dishwasher only when it is full.

✓ Use shorter cycles.

✓ Wash the largest items by hand, leaving room in the dishwasher for many small items.

✓ Turn off the dishwasher after the final rinse and open the door slightly to air dry the dishes. This saves up to 50 percent of the electricity used in a complete cycle.

✓ Keep the dishwasher filter screen clean.

Miscellaneous

✓ Thaw (or partly thaw) frozen foods in the fridge before cooking.

✓ It's more efficient to heat cold water on the stove than to run the water till it's hot and then boil it. Even in an efficient water heater, the water is constantly losing heat, especially when it is running through the pipes.

✓ An instant hot water appliance (installed at your sink) is as efficient as boiling water on the stove, unless the pot is small compared to the volume of water in it.

✓ Don't buy overspecialized gadgets that were built only to earn money for manufacturers.

✓ Bleached coffee filters and paper towels have dioxins, which are dangerous chemicals. Use unbleached or reusable filters.

✓ Use the smallest appropriate appliance.

✓ Don't wrap baked potatoes in aluminum foil. They don't need it. Cut them in half and microwave them face down on a plate or simply bake them unwrapped.

✓ Steam corn on the cob instead of boiling it. This uses less water and heating fuel. It's faster and the corn tastes better.

✓ If you eat meat, cook it in small pieces rather than whole roasts or birds. This uses less fuel.

✓ Use paper towels sparingly or not at all. Use cloth dishtowels instead.

✓ Enjoy more raw fresh foods (fruit, nuts, salads) that require no cooking at all.

Use water wisely

Water is far more important than gold. We can't live without it, yet we are rapidly exhausting our supplies due to overpopulation, over-consumption, pollution, waste, and agriculture.

- Agriculture uses two-thirds of the water being drawn from rivers, lakes, and aquifers—twice as much water as all buildings, industry, and mining combined.

- In 1998 the world ate 26 percent more meat than in 1990. Huge amounts of water are needed to grow crops for animals and to water the animals themselves.

- Manure and other runoff of pesticides, hormones, and antibiotics contaminate our waters. Such pollution wastes almost as much water as we actually use.

In response to shortages, the United States is dipping into our underground water, some of which was deposited eons ago as fossil water. The Ogallala aquifer is a huge underground reservoir in eight midwestern states that provides water for 20 percent of America's irrigated land. The Ogallala aquifer was being reduced 3 to 10 feet a year by 1990. It is now being depleted by 12 billion cubic meters a year.

What you can do

- ✓ Keep a bottle of drinking water in the fridge so that you won't have to run the tap to get cool water.

- ✓ Fix leaky faucets. Hot water leaks are doubly costly since you're also paying for heating.

- ✓ Don't turn on the tap and then wander around the kitchen peeking in the fridge or looking for dishes to wash.

- ✓ A faucet aerator reduces the water flow by half, although the flow will seem stronger.

- ✓ Eat less meat. If we all did so, the same volume of water could feed two people instead of one.

- ✓ It takes 1,000 tons of water to produce a ton of grain. So reduce your waste of grain foods.

✓ Resist the temptation to use running water as a "broom" in your kitchen sink or driveway.

✓ Don't use antibacterial soap. We are inadvertently creating superbugs resistant to antibiotics because we overuse them in medicines and soaps.

Is washing dishes by hand more environmentally friendly than using a dishwasher? It depends. When you're washing by hand, do you let the hot water run incessantly? Do you use so much soap that you have to use a lot of water to rinse it off? Do you let dishes sit for days before washing them, so that the food has crusted and requires repeated washing? All of these may mean you're not washing efficiently. Meanwhile, a dishwasher filled completely and run on an energy-conserving cycle can actually be efficient.

What you can do

✓ Don't pre-wash your dishes; just scrape them before putting them in the dishwasher.

✓ Don't let the faucet run at high volume you're while rinsing dishes one at a time.

✓ Compost the scraps instead of spending water and electricity to put them down the disposal.

✓ Run the dishwasher only when it's full. Each load uses up to 15 gallons of water (not to mention soap and the electricity to heat the water).

✓ Set your dishwasher on air dry so you don't use a lot of electricity to do something dishes will do all by themselves—dry!

Saving water on the farm

In 1980, before the A2 Water Management Act was passed, irrigation on farms was typically only 85 percent efficient. Responding to regulations, Arizona farmer Howard Wuertz started subsurface drip irrigation, watering only the root zone of plants. This is 95 percent efficient, and it cut costs, improved yields, and allowed the farmer to expand acreage and profits.

Use only good gadgets

Some kitchen tools are indispensable, others are useful, and some are toys. Gadgets save labor by using electricity to chop, puree, or cook things slowly or quickly or in a specialized way. Some gadgets seem designed to save muscle power, on the assumption that manual labor is somehow demeaning. But then we go to the gym to use fancy machines to build up our muscles. When you chop vegetables and open cans by hand, you are using less electricity. Think of how many gadgets sit gathering dust in cabinets, waiting for the day they are set out in a garage sale.

Every kitchen gadget contains materials such as metal, plastic, glass, paint, and petroleum. Manufacturing them also requires energy to dig the ore, and to heat, mix, and shape the materials. Finally, packaging and transporting products through distribution channels to your home takes energy. Experts call all this "embedded energy." Even the handle of a gadget represents many units of energy. Embedded energy is in all products, from cars to can openers, so choose your gadgets wisely. Pressure cookers (with tight-fitting lids that allow water to be super-heated above 212 degrees) do save energy. But manufacturing a new one involves embedded energy, so be sure you'll actually use it before investing in one. Better solution: get a used one at a garage sale or thrift shop.

Some kitchen gadgets are really toys for grownups: microwaveable ice cream scoops, for instance. If your ice cream is so hard that you can't scoop it, your freezer is too cold. Save energy and help the earth by turning up the freezer temperature a little. Hot dog warmers, bacon cookers, microwaveable hot plates, sandwich heating machines—we've even seen advertisements for home cotton candy making machines. Do you really need these things? Are they really welcome as gifts? Electric can openers are a bit more sensible—and valuable for those with physical impairments. But how often do you use one? Or that waffle iron?

What you can do

- ✓ Use the smallest practical appliance without compromising safety.
- ✓ Single-task appliances, such as waffle irons, should be purchased only if you will use them regularly.

- ✓ If you are concerned about the quality of your drinking water, you could invest in a water filter, in the form of a pitcher or a device that attaches to your tap. After recouping the initial embedded energy, the filter will save the resources that would be used to produce, package, and transport bottled water.
- ✓ Check the EPA's evaluation of the energy efficiency of appliances. Other companies and nonprofits also share this information.
- ✓ Buy some gadgets second-hand.
- ✓ Take care of your appliances so that they last longer.

Recycling mastery

When Syamavati, the queen consort of King Udayana, offered Ananda 500 garments, Ananda received them with great satisfaction. The king, hearing of it, suspected Ananda of dishonesty, so he went to Ananda and asked what he was going to do with these 500 garments. Ananda replied, "O king, many of the brothers are in rags; I am going to distribute the garments among the brothers."

"What will you do with the old garments?"

"We will make bedcovers out of them."

"What will you do with the old bedcovers?

"We will make pillow cases."

"What will you do with the old pillow cases?"

"We will make floor covers out of them."

"What will you do with the old floor covers?"

"We will use them for foot towels."

"What will you do with the old foot towels?"

"We will use them for floor-mops."

"What will you do with the old floor mops?"

"Your highness, we will tear them into pieces, mix them with mud, and use the mud to plaster the house walls."

Enjoy leftovers

Food that reaches your table represents planting, watering, outwitting the competition (bugs also want that berry or grain of wheat), harvesting, saving seeds for next year, packing, shipping, and marketing. If you've grown food yourself, you know the attention that went into it. If every American throws out one bite of beans with gravy, 8 million pounds of food are wasted, and 16 million pounds are lost if every American throws out one tablespoon of mashed potatoes. Help the earth by serving reasonable portions, following the motto, "Take what you like, eat what you take." What's left in the serving dishes can be turned into leftovers. Linda remembers the joke in her college dorm that Sunday suppers were "food of the week in review."

You probably already do some leftover performance art: Thanksgiving turkey provides sandwiches, casseroles, and soup for a week—longer if you boil the bones to make broth. We encourage you to do this more often. That untouched potato, half a cup of pasta sauce, and last half of a zucchini could be part of a wonderful soup. The French call it *pot au feu*—the pot on the fire where leftovers go for their next incarnation. It's fun—you end up with dishes that are never exactly the same and you get to exercise your creativity.

The way you store leftovers can also help the earth. Aluminum foil and cling wrap do save food, but they use metals and petrochemicals, and cause damage when they are extracted, manufactured, and discarded. So let's look at foil and wrap as the valuable commodities they are, not trash to be used once and thrown away.

What you can do

✓ Learn some new recipes.

✓ Take only what you'll eat.

✓ Check your fridge's crisper drawer so that you remember what's there. Use fresh produce promptly.

✓ Consider following the European custom—buy smaller amounts of fresh produce, and do so more often. Walk to the store. Less produce is wasted and you get some exercise and social contact.

✓ Put leftovers in a bowl and invert a saucer on top, using no foil or wrap at all.

✓ Reuse aluminum foil repeatedly before putting it in the recycle bin.

✓ Reuse cling wrap at least once, then return it to the supermarket to recycle.

✓ Store several items together—rice and vegetables, potatoes and beans—to minimize the use of foil and plastic.

✓ Reusable plastic containers with lids last for years.

✓ Use empty yogurt containers or other manufacturers' containers to store your leftovers.

The fourth R

Students and staff at the high school in Reeds Spring, Missouri, are salvaging food and paper from their 2,200 student school district. At a building near the high school, food waste from the cafeterias, wrappings, yard trimmings, and nonrecyclable paper are collected and processed, saving the district about $11,000 a year in waste disposal costs. The finished compost is sold and the proceeds used to help support the project and a scholarship fund. Meanwhile Santa Monica College in suburban Los Angeles found that food waste made up about 7% of the overall waste on campus. The college is conducting an experiment with vermicomposting. Discarded paper and food waste from the cafeteria are shredded and placed in a bin where 300 pounds of worms eat the waste and turn it into fertilizer.

Reduce waste

There is no waste in nature. Every plant, animal, rock, and drop of water is broken down and reused. Fallen trees provide homes for many species as they slowly decay and return to the soil. Fallen leaves, the shells left by a nut-eating squirrel, and the fur or feathers left by a predator are recycled in the ecosystem, decaying and becoming soil in which new plants and animals can live and grow. Rain forests are lush not because the soil is rich—it isn't—but because the plants decompose rapidly, returning their nutrients to the earth for the next generation. We humans have disturbed this cycle, taking unwanted material to landfills, where it is junked with old batteries, turpentine, plastic containers, and other unnatural trash to be sealed off for decades.

The amount of food we waste annually is staggering. One study found that we waste 96 billion pounds of food a year—about 27 percent of all the food produced. During World War II, it was considered patriotic to use everything thriftily, from food to gasoline to clothing. More than 20,000 committees and 400,000 volunteers organized to recycle metal, rubber, and other materials. In the urgency of war, we realized that natural resources were precious. They still are.

To reduce waste, we can serve ourselves consciously, reuse some things, compost the rest. Even the end of the food cycle—what's left after every bit of usable food has been eaten—can help restore the earth. Peels and plate scraps can go into the compost pile, while water from cooking vegetables can be cooled and put onto the houseplants. Your kitchen becomes a way station in the great cycle of life.

What you can do

- ✓ Overcome routine and impulse. Look beyond your usual selections, and have some idea what you'll do with the items you put in your basket.

- ✓ Don't be afraid of small imperfections. Most blemishes on fresh produce do not affect its taste or nutritional value. A tiny dot of mold on bread can be cut away.

- ✓ If you buy produce on sale, it's probably at the peak of ripeness and about to go bad soon. Eat it right away.

- ✓ Give yourself smaller servings. Tune in to your stomach: how hungry are you, really?

- ✓ Put leftovers in the front of the fridge so that you remember to use them.

Creative thinking

In Los Angeles, a local utility offered rebates on low-flow toilets to help conserve water. But low-income residents couldn't afford to pay their portion or to wait for the rebates. A partnership was formed with the utility, a corporation, and community groups. The corporation bought 1,000 low-flow toilets and gave them to community groups to give away. The recipients exchanged their old inefficient toilets, which were ground up to be put into road base. The citizens got new toilets, the utility saved water, and the old toilets were turned into roads.

Industrial-strength recycling

Xerox saved $45 million in 1998 by recycling or refurbishing 72,000 tons of old machines. It also offers a new efficient copier that is 97 percent recyclable. Remanufacturing is expected to save the company over $1 billion. Meanwhile, the Bank of America reconditioned 35,000 pieces of equipment, saving $7 million. Such positive results for the bottom line might encourage other manufacturers to reclaim used products.

Share the bounty

So you've saved leftovers for creative reuse and sent scraps and peels to the compost. Is there anything more you can do? You could help hungry people in your community. Thirty-four thousand children a day die from hunger or preventable diseases linked to hunger. One in six persons worldwide is malnourished, including 160 million children under the age of 5. Twenty to thirty million Americans are too poor to buy enough food compatible with health, and some of them live near you. In the back of your cupboard cans of food are probably nearing their expiration date. A food bank could use these. You may have backyard produce. There are millions of fruit trees in this country, and many of them are not being fully harvested. An organization called Second Harvest will come to your house and collect the apples and pears that might otherwise go to waste. Huge amounts of food get lost in the cracks of distribution. Fortunately, an Internet site connects relief agencies with food supplies. See *www.resourcelink.hp.com*.

What you can do

✓ Donate canned goods to food banks.

✓ Unopened baked goods can be donated to local food banks or holiday drives.

✓ Contact Second Harvest to gather the crops from your fruit trees that might otherwise be wasted, *www.secondharvest.org*.

✓ Patronize restaurants that participate in food banks.

✓ Donate leftovers to food banks.

How many miles per tablespoon?

Ordinary cooking oil is being turned into fuel for automobiles. With minimal adaptation, a car can run on vegetable oil which can be easily processed with lye and methanol. The fuel gives off lower emissions (no benzene or sulfur, less carbon monoxide and hydrocarbons). It is carbon neutral, biodegradable, and easily produced domestically.

Clean up harmlessly

Cleaning up after meals can be hard on the earth if you throw away a lot of paper and use harsh chemical and abrasive cleansers. Paper towels can be handy, but use them sparingly. We've seen people tear off a sheet, use it to wipe up a few drops of spilled tea, and throw it away. Cascading helps a bit, but using cloth is even better. Using a cloth dishtowel to wipe your hands and countertops instead of using three paper towels a day saves 10 pounds of paper towel a year. If every U.S. household did this, we could save 30,000 trees every year.

The same holds true for cloth napkins. If a family of four used cloth napkins at every meal for a year, they would save 4,380 paper napkins from the landfill. There is some laundering involved, but cloth napkins are an inexpensive, simple way to reduce your household's trash and help the earth.

Earth-friendly papers with more recycled content are available. According to Seventh Generation, a Vermont provider of household goods (including 100 percent recycled paper towels), if every household in America replaced one roll of 180-sheet, two-ply, virgin fiber paper towels with a 100 percent recycled one, we would save 864,000 trees, 3.4 million cubic feet of landfill (or 3,900 full garbage trucks), and 354 million gallons of water (a year's supply for 10,100 families of four). You could also look for rolls that have half-size sheets, which are useful for small jobs.

Alternatives to harsh cleansers full of phosphorus, chemicals, perfumes, dyes, and abrasive powders are available in stores, or you could devise your own. Baking soda, vinegar, and ammonia can be used to clean many things. Annie Berthold Bond maintains that five basic materials will clean everything: baking soda, washing soda, distilled white vinegar, vegetable-based liquid soap, and tea tree oil. *Hints from Heloise* offers ideas for turning familiar household items into materials for storage and cleaning.

What you can do

✓ Combine half a cup of white vinegar with enough water to make a gallon. This can be used to clean dishes, coffeepots, etc.

✓ A solution of half vinegar and half water is strong enough to clean refrigerator doors and handles.

✓ Baking soda is a good abrasive for appliances, cutting boards, and sinks, and it deodorizes at the same time.

✓ If food has burned in a pot or pan, soak it before scrubbing. You could even put it back on the burner to boil with the soaking water. For badly charred stainless steel pots, pour in full-strength vinegar and let it stand for several days.

✓ As a preventive measure, add a bit of vinegar to the water for boiling potatoes or eggs to brighten the pan.

✓ **WARNING: Never combine ammonia with chlorine. This creates dangerous fumes**

The Environmental Protection Agency recommends these techniques:

✓ Instead of using harsh oven cleaner chemicals and a huge jolt of electricity, clean oven spills with baking soda and steel wool before they harden. Add salt if the stain is especially tough.

✓ If a drain is clogged, use a plumber's snake or plunger instead of dangerous chemicals.

✓ To polish silver, use nonabrasive toothpaste.

The Alameda County, California, Clean Water Program adds:

✓ Use vinegar and water to remove residue from baking soda.

✓ Use all-purpose vegetable-based liquid soap.

✓ Avoid products with silica and chlorine.

✓ Prevent oven spills; clean them up promptly when they occur.

Maximize materials by recycling

You're probably already recycling some of the paper, aluminum, steel, glass, and plastic that comes into your life. It's even possible to install kitchen cabinets with built-in recycling bins. But we can do better.

- Almost half of used paper now is recycled, but about 44 million tons are still discarded in the U.S. each year. This is more than all the paper used in China annually.

- Every three months, the United States discards enough aluminum to rebuild the American commercial airline fleet and enough steel to completely rebuild the cities of Chicago and New York.

- Americans use 2.5 million plastic bottles every hour.

Recycling helps the earth. Recycling one ton of office paper reduces solid waste by 49 percent, energy use by 43 percent, greenhouse gases by 70 percent, hazardous air pollution by 90 percent, particulate emissions by 40 percent, absorbable organic halogen emissions to water by 100 percent, and suspended solids by 30 percent. Each ton of recycled paper also saves 17 trees, 64 gallons of oil, 42 gallons of gasoline, 4,210 kilowatt hours of power, 7,000 gallons of water, and 3.5 cubic yards of landfill space. Recycling paper reduces water use by 60 percent, energy by 70 percent, and pollution by half. Recycling creates 100 jobs for every 13 lost. Nationwide, there are 45,000 recycling jobs. Recycling also helps cities and states save money.

- In eight years, Madison, Wisconsin, tripled its diversion of residential solid waste, decreasing costs from $158 to $139 per household. Mesa, Arizona, saved over $650,000 annually.

- A city of one million people could save $57 million by operating a single mill to process 100,000 tons of used newspaper, or it could spend $4 million to dispose of it. That's a big swing. What could your city do with $57 million?

Of course, recycling isn't a free lunch, and it isn't perfect. We still have to use energy to move the material and process it. Supply and demand are not perfectly matched. But recycling is the most immediate and sensible way citizens can help lighten our load on the earth.

What you can do

- ✓ Recycle glass, aluminum, paper, newspaper, and plastic.

- ✓ Carry bottles and cans home from your workplace or ball park if they don't have recycling bins. Encourage them to get bins.

- ✓ Buy goods made from recycled materials—paper, fleece parkas, plastic trash bags, shoes, garden tools, carpets and carpet pads, and more. This encourages manufacturers to buy the "waste" material and turn it into new products.

- ✓ Eat less fast food. Brown bag lunch from home instead.

- ✓ If you do go to a fast food establishment, tell the manager you're concerned about recycling. Write letters to corporate headquarters.

- ✓ Support state and local laws and ordinances requiring good waste management practices.

Swords into topsoil

When an army base, the Presidio in San Francisco, was converted to park use, the planners decided to add composting to their operations. 40% of available organic materials, such as yard trimmings, wood materials, and manure are being composted. Schoolchildren on field trips help staffers sift, turn, and make compost piles. The finished product is distributed to a nearby golf course and used to help restore native vegetation.

Build topsoil by composting

The next stop on your food's march through your kitchen is the compost heap. We've mentioned that America's topsoil, the layer of earth in which we grow our crops, is being lost at an alarming rate. Topsoil is the stuff of life, the very source of plants on which humans and animals ultimately depend. Ancient peoples knew the value of soil, yet apparently we don't. Tons of precious earth are floating down the Mississippi River and our other rivers and streams or blowing away in the wind.

- In the United States, a third of our original topsoil is gone. 90 percent of U.S. farmland is losing topsoil faster than new soil is being formed—on average, 17 times faster.

- Items sent to landfills do not turn into dirt, at least not in our lifetimes. Organic matter is discarded along with chemicals, turpentine, plastics, and other nondegradable material. Cabbages, carrots, and readable newspapers have remained recognizable for 30 years or more.

Why does this matter? Modern agricultural methods destroy soil. Topsoil is blown away or swept down rivers and out to sea. Agricultural practices that lead to erosion include overgrazing, monoculture, row cropping, tilling, and plowing. Each year 12 to 16 million acres of productive land are lost worldwide. Arable land is also being lost to erosion, salinization, urban sprawl, and desertification faster than land is being brought into cultivation.

Individuals can do something about this. Food and yard wastes make up approximately 30 percent of the waste stream in the United States. Once you start composting, you'll be amazed that you ever thought of food scraps as garbage. To make a compost heap, you could simply make a pile in the yard, or you could purchase a bin from the local hardware store or home supply warehouse. Some cities subsidize bins, making them available to local residents at a deep discount. There are bin designs for every budget and level of interest. There's even a small one you can keep in the house.

When your bin is set up, simply drop your kitchen waste in it whenever enough has accumulated. Your grass clippings and other yard waste can also go here, and so can an amazing variety of other things:

vacuum cleaner lint, wool and cotton rags, sawdust, wilted flowers, fireplace ashes, and biodegradable picnic utensils. Properly tended, a compost heap can turn this material into new earth in a few weeks. To speed up the process, you can add a little nitrogen-rich manure purchased from the hardware store, stir the heap occasionally, and put in some worms. These trusty creatures gobble up the leftovers and turn them into dirt. Compost aficionados describe the fine points of layering, nitrogen concentration, moisture levels, and turning frequency as other ways to speed up the process. You can do all that, but it isn't required. Time alone will turn your scraps into black gold.

Municipalities, corporations, and smaller businesses are realizing the benefits of composting. There are already 3,500 commercial composting facilities, and some local businesses are composting, too.

- Composting can divert an average of 700 pounds of material per household per year from the waste stream.

- On average, communities with backyard compost programs gain more than $3.50 in direct, measurable benefits for every $1 invested in the program.

- The payback period for a homeowner buying his or her own compost bin is less than a year in Marion County, Oregon.

- Seattle gives away compost bins and saves nearly $18 per ton by diverting organics through its backyard composting program instead of land filling.

- Composting could lighten the burden agriculture places on the earth, leading to improved soil and yields, higher resistance to pests, reduced erosion and runoff, reduced workers' exposure to pesticides, and savings in water and the energy used to pump water. Then there are financial benefits. It's been estimated that if more agricultural leftovers were composted, $132 million could be saved in California alone.

Composting is an easy, inexpensive way to renew the earth. As the Alameda County, California, waste board says, "Do the rot thing!" You'll be surprised how much lovely vegetable matter you can personally save from the dump. Whenever you compost instead of using the disposal, you're also saving water and electricity. Plus, your trash bill might go down if a smaller garbage can will now fit your needs. With your home-made dirt, you can improve the soil on your property or give it away to friends. And you'll have the satisfaction of knowing you are returning to the age-old cycle of soil to food to soil.

What you can do

- ✓ Save potato peels, apple cores, banana peels, soggy lettuce leaves—all those things that never make it to your table.

- ✓ Add the scrapings from your plates after meals (except meat, dairy, and eggs, which might attract animals).

- ✓ Keep an empty milk carton or used plastic bag in the sink to collect scraps. Some people prefer a special crock for this purpose.

- ✓ Some picnic utensils are biodegradable.

- ✓ If you're doing a big job like cleaning seeds out of a pumpkin or coring two dozen apples, put a sheet of newspaper on the counter to collect the leavings. Then you can wrap up the whole bundle and take it to your compost pile, though purists might disapprove of the ink.

Gourmet dirt

San Francisco is conducting a pilot program to collect food waste from its 6,000 restaurants and turn it into compost. The restaurants' scraps are combined with yard waste and straw from a nearby veterinary school. The end product is high in nitrogen and is expected to be sold as soil amendment. Greg Pryor, manager of the landfill where the food scraps are taken and transformed into fertilizer, says, "It's black gold."

PART III

Away from Home

ALL OVER THE WORLD there are people who have entered into the exercise of imagining a sustainable world. They can see it as a world to move toward not reluctantly, not with a sense of sacrifice or regret, but joyfully. It could be a very much better world than the one we live in today.

—Donella Meadows, Dennis Meadows, and Jorgen Randers

Dining out

Americans are a mobile people. We relocate, we travel, we dine out a lot. Collectively, we spend almost half our food dollars and consume about half our daily calories away from home. We eat at fast food establishments, sit-down restaurants, in our cars, outdoors, at work, at play, and while traveling. Dining out represents a $399 billion market, amounting to 4 percent of the gross domestic product. We spend $1.1 billion dining out on a typical day.

Some sit-down restaurants serve large portions, and they're getting larger. What to do? Eating everything on the plate may make us overweight. Taking home leftovers prevents food waste but creates packaging waste, since leftovers are wrapped in foil or put into styrofoam or a paper bag, sometimes several of these—even an "elegant" sculpted foil swan.

We could eat less. Across the world, 850 million to 1 billion people a day are hungry, while 600 million are overfed and overweight. World Watch Institute concluded, "As calorie-rich junk foods squeeze healthy items from the diet, obesity often masks nutrient starvation ... [People are] essentially trading diseases of dietary deficiency for diseases of dietary excess." This is called "affluent malnutrition."

- In the United States, fat and sugar make up over half our caloric intake. Whole grains have been replaced by refined ones, and 20 percent of what we call vegetables are actually fries and chips.

- Fifty-five percent of adults in the U.S. are overweight. Almost a quarter of Americans are obese, up from 15 percent in 1980. One in five American children is overweight or obese, a 50 percent increase in the same time period.

- Obesity creates medical costs of $118 billion annually, more than twice the costs caused by cigarettes. In addition, we spend $33 billion on diet drugs and weight-loss products and programs.

What you can do when dining at sit-down restaurants

✓ Ask the staff to remove the bread and butter if you don't want it.

✓ Order only what you can eat.

✓ Share a main course if you're not very hungry.

✓ Take home leftovers. One survey found that over half of restaurant diners do so, almost a third split a single main course, and an eighth ask for half orders.

✓ Ask the server to omit things you don't eat (pickles, sour cream, potato chips).

✓ Ask your local restaurants to use unbleached napkins, to recycle and compost, and to serve some vegetarian options.

✓ Tell the waiter (and the manager and owner) why you chose the restaurant and why you're choosing your earth-friendly entrée.

Fast food restaurants have not been doing well by the earth, offering packaging and food that have been factory-processed and trucked long distances. The large chains have enormous power over the food supply, encourage monoculture and cruel factory farming of animals, and make decisions based on profit. We spent over $110 billion on fast food in 2000. This is more than we spent on higher education, personal computers, software, or new cars. It is more than we spent on books, movies, magazines, newspapers, videos, and recorded music combined. McDonald's is the nation's largest purchase of beef and potatoes, and the second largest purchaser of chicken.

On the other hand, when it does respond to consumer pressure, the fast food industry's decisions can be beneficial on a large scale. McDonald's recently bowed to protests and started requiring its suppliers to treat cows, pigs, and chickens more humanely. This will impact the industry widely.

What you can do in fast food establishments

✓ Consider patronizing an independent fast-food restaurant.

✓ Avoid the drive-through windows, especially if there is a long line of cars ahead of you. This is sedentary and can waste gas.

✓ Order only what you can eat.

✓ Get only the condiments that you'll use.

✓ Don't take or accept more napkins than you need.

✓ Encourage establishments to start serving vegeburgers. Then order them!

✓ Be aware of which fast food chains are beginning to take action to reduce their environmental impact.

✓ Tell management you have concerns about the environmental impacts of their restaurants.

Local flavor

In Tucson, Arizona, the Café Poca Cosa emphasizes locally grown food. Local farms supply the familiar onions, garlic, peppers, and eggplant, and also southwest specialties like prickly pear cactus, tomatillos, and cilantro. If they can feed themselves locally with less than 10 inches of rain a year, other parts of the country should be able to do so as well.

Support green restaurants

Some chefs and restaurateurs are exercising environmental aware-ness. At the White Dog Café in Philadelphia, owner Judy Wicks uses alternative energy such as windmill power for 44 percent of her energy, buys local and organic food, takes customers on eco-tours focusing on themes like alternative energy and urban sprawl, and holds farmer Sunday suppers to introduce her customers to the farm-ers who grow their food. Table talks are given at Monday night din-ners, with an invited speaker, and discussions of factory farming, genetically modified food, and diet choices and cancer. Benefits are held at outdoor buffets to help inner-city gardens or the Chef's Collaborative. The White Dog Café is truly a friend of the earth.

The Chef's Collaborative is a network of chefs, restaurateurs, and other food professionals working to promote sustainable agri-culture, support local farms, and educate us about clean, healthy food. The Chef's Collaborative has chapters nationwide and offers information on the Internet on which seafood species are endan-gered and should not be served. Among their principles are the fol-lowing:

- Good food begins with unpolluted air, land, and water, environmentally sustainable farming and fishing, and humane animal husbandry.

- Sound food choices emphasize locally grown, seasonally fresh, and whole or minimally processed ingredients.

- Cultural and biological diversity is essential for the health of the planet and its inhabitants. Preserving and revitalizing sustainable food and agricultural traditions strengthen that diversity.

- The healthy, traditional diets of many cultures offer abundant evi-dence that fruits, vegetables, beans, breads, and grains are the foundation of good diets.

There may be green restaurants in your area as well. If not, you can help develop them by communicating with waiters and owners when-ever you dine. Introduce them to the Chef's Collaborative. Investigate local restaurants in your community and patronize those with earth-friendly values. Green restaurants do some or all of the following:

- Serve a diverse selection of foods

- Offer vegetarian and vegan options

- Support the Chef's Collaborative commitment to serve only sustainable fish
- Purchase local ingredients from organic growers
- Offer varying portion sizes to discourage overeating
- Compost
- Recycle
- Donate to soup kitchens
- Have a children's menu so that small portions are available for small people

For some people, driving across town or to the middle of nowhere is part of the dining event. Unfortunately, it pours gasoline emissions into the air. Consider patronizing establishments closer to home, carpooling to that great restaurant, or saving it for special occasions.

What you can do

✓ Patronize green restaurants. Vegetarian restaurants and those near colleges and universities may be especially earth-conscious.

✓ Encourage other restaurants to become green.

✓ Patronize local restaurants.

✓ Choose locally grown foods.

Caterers

You or your workplace might order a catered event—an office party, wedding, anniversary, or fund-raiser for a volunteer organization. If you arrange events frequently or if you're a food or hospitality professional, you could become especially knowledgeable about the green caterers in your area, or educate them to become green. Many caterers are small local businesses. You can influence them because, in hiring them, you are the boss. Ask the caterer to supply food that is organic, diverse, local, and prepared efficiently. Ask for little or no meat; if there is meat, it's farmed free or organic; and no endangered species. Green caterers also:

- Share unserved food with food banks, if allowed. Laws regulate commercial food preparation and disposal.

- Compost the scraps (or collect them so that you can compost them).

- Use reusable or compostable utensils.

- Use paper goods made from recycled paper.

- Clean up afterwards using kinder cleansers, unbleached paper, and recycling.

Your role is to help estimate the amount of food needed. This will depend on the nature of the event (wedding or baseball tournament, buffet or sit-down dinner?), the number of guests likely to attend, what time of day (mealtime or after school?), the age and activity level of the guests (seniors or teenagers?), and other factors that a knowledgeable caterer will encourage you to consider. You don't want to run out of food, and it's unlikely that you'll serve the precise amount the party consumes; you'll probably have a surplus. Consider this when you plan an event so that extras can be taken home, saved for the next day, or donated to food banks. If you are the organizer of a club's or charity's regular events (fund-raising benefits, annual sporting tournaments), keep records on how much and what kind of food the people in your group tend to eat. You can also buy computer software to help you estimate quantities and select recipes based on preferred ingredients. The caterer will help you estimate quantities.

What you can do

✓ Carefully estimate the amount of food you need. If you are worried about falling short, ask the caterer to have a backup item in reserve. You pay for this item; if it is not served, you can take it home.

✓ Compare the environmental impact of renting china and tableware with the impact of disposable plates and utensils. If you choose the latter, make sure they're biodegradable.

✓ Arrange the timing of food preparation and serving so that less is wasted.

✓ Coordinate with the caterer to control the temperature of preparing and holding food.

Delicious and green, too

Berkeley's Urban Kitchen caterers had been in business for six months when we interviewed owners Sascha Weiss and Ann Dunn. They use organic produce because it tastes better and because they want to support organic farmers and the health of the workers who pick the produce. They buy cleaning products and trash bags with the environment in mind. All this costs a bit more and they lose a few prospective customers, but they gain other customers who are relieved to find that they can hold festive events without harming earth. Cooking for the health of person and planet is not about sacrifice or enduring boring food, Weiss and Dunn state firmly. "We've never done an event without someone coming up to us and saying, 'I'm not a vegetarian, but if I could cook like this, I would be'."

Avoid endangered species

One of the things that surprised us most when we were doing research for this book was how much sea life is threatened by human fishing and eating habits. Not just whales and dolphins, but also fish of many kinds are sinking in numbers, as are mollusks (such as squids) and crustaceans (such as lobsters). We were also surprised that the apparent solution—aquaculture as it is now practiced—created problems.

- It can take decades for a fish population to recover from over-fishing. Fourteen major species in the U.S. are so seriously depleted they'll need 5 to 20 years to recover, even if all fishing of them stopped now.

- We've consumed so many of the large fish that we're now going lower on the food chain. The experts who studied this concluded, "If the trend continues, more and more regions are likely to experience complete collapse of their fisheries."

- The average American eats two and a half pounds of shrimp every year. Most are farmed in Asia and Latin America by methods that clear cut mangrove forests, poison bays and estuaries, and impoverish people living in coastal area.

Environmental facts are constantly changing, partly due to worsening conditions, but sometimes due to successes. Some species have been taken off the endangered species list, while others have been added. Swordfish, for example, have benefited from protection and are less endangered. A two-year campaign to stop the eating of swordfish, started by SeaWeb and the Natural Resources Defense Council and supported by 700 chefs nationwide, has been lifted.

What you can do

- ✓ Keep up to date on what's endangered. See the websites we recommend above in our Fish section.

- ✓ For now, avoid swordfish, orange roughy, grouper, atlantic cod, haddock, yellowtail, flounder, monkfish, and scallops.

- ✓ Tell restaurants why you are avoiding endangered fish.

✓ Encourage restaurants and caterers to join the Chef's Collaborative.

✓ Try vegetarian dishes.

A new Pacific haven

Palmyra Atoll, a cluster of uninhabited islets south of Hawaii, was purchased by the Nature Conservancy in 2000 and has become a marine sanctuary where sea life can survive undisturbed by industry or commercial fishing. The Nature Conservancy, one of the largest conservation organizations in the United States, has protected more than 12 million acres in the country, and works internationally with partners to save land overseas.

Outdoor lovers live up to their goals

Patagonia, which manufactures outdoor clothing and gear, donates 1 percent of sales to environmental groups and helps publicize environmental campaigns such as removing outdated dams. Patagonia uses only organic cotton in their clothing. This is significant because cotton is one of the most pesticide-intensive products on the market. Patagonia also heats its plants by recirculating hot water, using motion detectors to reduce light use, and has bathroom countertops made of recycled bottles.

Picnics and camping

Outdoor eating is familiar to us all, from sandwiches on benches outside our workplaces to picnics in a local park and barbecues in the back yard. Sometimes "away from home" means really away—camping in the woods. Twenty million Americans are active campers. Yet we make a mess of the very places we travel so far to admire, leaving behind our bottles, papers, and other trash. We throw food away rather than carry it home, accustoming wild animals to finding food in waste bins or thrown on the ground. This is not safe for them or for us! We may also buy highly processed and packaged convenience foods to take on our "nature" hikes. Remember the outdoor-lover's motto: "Take nothing but pictures and memories; leave nothing but footprints."

What you can do

✓ Bring reusable utensils and then take them away with you.

✓ If you must use disposable plates, utensils, and cups, use biodegradable ones.

✓ Don't use lighter fluid to start the barbecue. Lighter fluid contributes to smog—half a ton of it a day in the large metropolitan area around San Francisco.

✓ Use a chimney starter, a metal cylinder with a handle into which you put your charcoal briquettes. They heat up much faster and require no lighter fluid.

✓ Corn on the cob can be grilled in its husk if you first soak the husk in water. This eliminates the need for aluminum foil.

✓ If you use charcoal briquettes, douse them after you're done cooking. This helps prevent fires, and briquette pieces make good fixings to start the next fire.

✓ Put leftovers in reusable containers.

✓ Recycle everything recyclable and properly dispose of all litter.

✓ True eco-heroes even clean up the litter left behind by others.

At work, at play, and on the run

On any given day 141 million Americans are at work. The second most popular place to have breakfast is in the car. On an average day, almost 21 million people travel on airplanes. Theme parks log over 300 million visits a year, where people spend $9.1 billion, much of it on food. The 185 accredited zoos and aquariums in this country log over 134 million visits a year, more than all professional football, baseball, and basketball games combined.

Ecotourism—traveling to beautiful locations to enjoy the places and animals—gives incentives to people to preserve their lands. A lion living for seven years in Kenya is worth $515,000 in ecotourism but only $1,000 if it is killed for its skin. In Texas, the Laguna Atascosa National Wildlife Refuge recieves almost 500,000 visitors annually, pumping $100 million into the local economy. Working vacations are also possible. With such groups as Earthwatch and Global Volunteers, you can spend a few weeks assisting researchers who study dozens of environmental topics.

What you can do at work

✓ Brown bag your meals more often. Bring leftovers from home in reusable containers, or recycle the brown bag. With reusable cloth or plastic lunch containers, you can enjoy your leftovers, reduce packaging, and save money. This is especially easy if you have a microwave oven in your workplace.

✓ Bring only what you can eat.

✓ Bring washable plates, cups, and utensils you can leave at your workplace, especially your own coffee mug.

✓ Recycle.

✓ Encourage the company cafeteria to serve earth friendly and vegetarian options, and then select them.

What you can do when commuting, at play, or on the run:

✓ When buying a small item (one muffin) ask the clerk not to put it in a bag.

✓ At theme parks, ballparks, or zoo canteens, choose vegetarian options.

✓ Dispose of packaging properly.

What you can do on an airplane:

✓ Order special meals (such as vegetarian) in advance of the flight.

✓ Offer the food you do not want to neighboring passengers.

✓ Realize that the meals not eaten are disposed of by the airlines at the end of the flight. You can take some items (wrapped cookies or rolls) with you.

It's a wrap

A Michigan furniture manufacturer, Herman Miller Inc., saves $1.4 million a year by cleverly rethinking packaging methods. They created packing containers made of recycled detergent and milk containers that are reusable 80 to 100 times. They also use cartonless packaging, putting cardboard edges on corners of some furniture and then wrapping them in plastic film. Later they reuse the edges and recycle the plastic. This saves $250,000 a year for just one type of product.

Packaging again

Remember why packaging is so important—it literally strips the earth of soil, water, plants, and minerals and transfers them to landfills or roadsides. A person who uses styrofoam cups for a daily cup of coffee will, in the course of a year, make a pile of discarded cups 120 feet tall. If 280 million Americans did the same, the pile would be 6.35 million miles, which is 366 times around the earth. Meanwhile, two to three tons of trees are needed to make one ton of paper and 48 percent of all paper goes to packaging. The costs are soil erosion, species lost when land is cleared of trees, air pollution from pulp mills and waste incinerators, and dioxin released by mills. The world loses 30 million acres of forest a year.

Since every type of packaging has drawbacks, there are always trade-offs. Plantations of trees, which would seem to address the deforestation problem, are monocultures that require fertilizers, herbicides, and pesticides. Sometimes it's hard to know what is the best choice. We can only do our best, realizing that we don't have perfect solutions yet. The ultimate goal is to reduce disposable packaging, replacing it with reusable kinds.

What you can do:

- ✓ At parties where disposable cups are used, write people's names on them so that they can use only one cup each throughout the evening.

- ✓ At picnics, use reusable plastic containers and dispose of trash properly.

- ✓ When brown bagging your meal, use cloth lunch bags instead of paper.

- ✓ Reuse the plastic bag your fresh produce came in. Then recycle it.

- ✓ Wash and reuse glass jars to carry food.

PART IV

Food for Thought

WE ARE NEVER OUTSIDE THE NATURAL WORLD, no matter where we live or what we do. The great challenge of modernity is to remember, in the face of all that tempts us to forget, just how interconnected the world is.

—William Cronon

Are the dangers real?

Let's take a closer look at some of the environmental threats facing the earth. *Global warming,* also called climate change, is the rise in the earth's average temperatures. It is caused by an increase in certain compounds, such as methane and carbon dioxide, that accumulate in the atmosphere. They are called greenhouse gases because they are in gas form and act like the heat-trapping layer of glass in a greenhouse. Warm air holds more water than cool air, causing the fresh water we rely on in rivers, underground reservoirs, and rainfall to be held in the air as vapor. This contributes to droughts and water shortages. Global warming also alters the air and water circulation patterns that create climate. El Nino is the best-known example of this.

Global warming during the last 25 years has been greater than in any period since measurement began. It has helped drive the tripling of natural weather disasters (floods, hurricanes) in the last decade; these are predicted to cost $300 billion a year in the near future. The arctic polar ice cap is melting and has thinned by 45 percent in the last four decades.

The United States is the leading maker of greenhouse gases. Although we account for only 5 percent of the world's population, we are responsible for about 20 percent of global warming. Global warming could fundamentally alter one-third of plant and animal habitats and lead to extinction of some plant and animal species.

Ozone, a form of oxygen, exists in two places. The ozone layer is a beneficial part of the upper atmosphere that forms the earth's outermost "skin" and protects us from ultraviolet radiation. If this layer disappears, life as we know it will be impossible. Pollution from factories, cars, and farm runoff has already drifted upward and created a rapidly growing hole in the ozone over Antarctica. Human health problems are already being caused by the thinning ozone layer, including skin cancer, eye cataracts, and weakened immune systems. At lower levels in the atmosphere, ozone forms smog and other pollutants that contribute to global warming.

Pesticides and herbicides are, by definition, poisons intended to kill insects and plants we don't like. We use millions of tons of pesticides each year, most of which end up in soil, air, water, food crops, and the bodies of humans and animals who eat these crops. *Antibiotics* are designed to kill harmful bacteria, but a few bacteria survive each dose and produce hardier offspring. In response, we invent stronger antibiotics. In this arms race against germs, we're overusing antibiotics (overmedicating ourselves and even putting them in soaps) to the point that antibiotics are losing their power. Medical authorities are alarmed at the prospect of untreatable superbug epidemics.

Air and water quality deteriorate as we load the atmosphere with chemicals and exhaust from cars, factories, and farm runoff. These materials don't go away; they return as acid rain or accumulate in the soil and water, ultimately ending up in the bodies of animals and humans. Asthma, infertility, cancer, and other health problems have been linked to chemical exposure.

When we clear-cut forests (either to use the trees for lumber and paper, or to clear the land for housing and farming), the tree roots holding the soil in place die. This allows soil erosion and subsequent flooding because the soil cannot absorb as much rainfall as before. This *deforestation* also destroys the habitat of woodland creatures and removes nature's best device for producing oxygen and disposing of carbon dioxide. *Topsoil depletion* occurs on the uppermost few inches of the earth's crust, which is the irreplaceable bed for plant life on which all animals and humans depend. Our machine-based agricultural methods loosen and disperse soil, which floats away on wind and streams; what's left is an exhausted residue laden with agricultural chemicals.

We are causing *extinctions of species,* by destroying their habitats to build cities, or by stripping soil for mining and factories, or by poisoning their habitats (as Rachel Carson found in *Silent Spring*), or by disrupting their food supply. Because of human activities, plants and animals are now vanishing 100 to 1,000 times faster than they would otherwise. At least 6,500 species are endangered in the United States alone. Many people think animals and natural places have a right to exist, just as we do. Furthermore, indigenous people may need the threatened plants and animals. There are other impacts: if one part of an ecosystem goes, the whole web could unravel; we might eliminate plants that could provide future medicines or substances; and genetic diversity is lost. Without diversity, one blight could kill an entire crop (as happened in Ireland in the nineteenth century, when a potato blight caused the starvation of millions of people) and inbreeding could occur (which creates health problems in animals and humans).

Food safety has become front-page news, in the forms of mad cow disease, foot-and-mouth disease, genetic modification of foods, and irradiation, not to mention unsanitary conditions and lax inspection in slaughterhouses. Diseases in the animals we raise for food are caused or spread by their living conditions, the food they eat, and how their bodies are slaughtered and handled. Genetic modification, which involves inserting genes from one species into another (tobacco genes into mice, for instance), has been linked to harm to wildlife. Irradiation is a last-ditch effort to kill pathogens when other measures have failed or have not been enforced, and its long-term effects on human health are unknown. These problems are part and parcel of the industrialization of the food supply.

Finally, we risk complete *exhaustion of natural resources*. Oil, water, and mineral ores are becoming harder to find. We are even considering drilling for oil in the Arctic, with irreparable damage to land, rivers, and animals. We could easily avoid this drilling by making our vehicles more efficient. Conflicts over water exist in some countries and are expected to get worse. Bauxite, from which aluminum is made, is found in tropical countries, so we chop down more rain forest to get the ore to make aluminum for soda cans and foil wrap. As former Wisconsin senator Gaylord Nelson said, "We are managing our planet as if it were a business in liquidation."

How could we have let things get to such a state? The news is scary. It's tempting to hope the problems will all go away. We may deny, minimize, or rationalize. Let's look at some of these responses.

1. There's no problem—it's all hysteria. There are plenty of people who dispute the warnings about the environment, saying the problems have been exaggerated. Keep in mind, however, that some people who deny the problems are motivated by economic gain. Generally, corporations simply don't want to admit and pay for the damages they cause, and they twist legitimate scientific disagreements into reasons to claim the problems don't exist. For example, a recent report warning of global warming, issued by thousands of scientists from over 100 countries, was attacked by 15 industry groups, including the National Mining

Association, the National Association of Manufacturers, and the American Petroleum Institute. The television program 20/20 criticized the safety of organic food without disclosing that a critic they featured had financial ties to agribusiness and chemical giants Monsanto, Dow AgroSciences, and AgroEvo and that their correspondent had agribusiness investments. The Fertilizer Institute funded a study which conveniently concluded that fertilizer runoff was not to blame for dead zones in the Gulf of Mexico. The USDA's new rules for labeling organic foods (which took 10 years to develop) have been criticized by grocery industry groups who don't want people to think they imply that organic is safer or healthier.

Such tactics have been used before. To say that the environmental dangers are not proven is to repeat the same kinds of denials made by the tobacco industry in the last thirty years. Tobacco interests, using outright lies, delays, smoke screens, and political campaign contributions, convinced enough people that the dangers of smoking were unproven so that they have been able to remain in business and unregulated to this day. This, despite the fact that 400,000 Americans a year

... RIGHT BEFORE OUR EYES...

Mutts cartoons reprinted with special permission of King Feature Syndicate

die from tobacco-related illnesses.

2. Extinctions are part of nature, so there's nothing to worry about. If one species goes extinct, another will evolve to fill the niche. It's evolution. Let's assume we decide to let some species go extinct because of our activities. Though insects can evolve rapidly, it can take thousands of years for larger species to evolve. Occasionally there have been "explosions" of new species, but this evolution is considered rapid only in geologic time, which is measured in millions of years. We would not live to see it happen. Do we want (and do we have the right) to create vacancies in nature, without knowing the outcome?

When a species disappears, a whole food web could collapse, or an ecosystem could deteriorate. When one member of a community disappears, there are ripple effects we are just beginning to understand. Look what happened when we overexploited one kind of fish in Alaska. Humans are catching three times as much pollock as in the mid-1980s. Steller's sea lions (which eat pollock) lost 90 percent of their population, which took away the main food source of killer whales. Killer whales then began to eat sea otters. Sea otter populations have declined by 90 percent since 1990. Sea urchins, now less threatened by sea otters, are multiplying.

3. We don't need to preserve vast tracts of natural land. Actually, we do. There are 6,500 endangered species in the United States, and others that will become endangered unless we change our ways. It's expensive to rescue an endangered species, and we can't create enough programs to save species one at a time. Their niches are complex and their biological needs are not fully understood. Some breed slowly in captivity, or not at all. The most efficient way to save nature and its creatures (including ourselves) is to save their dwelling places. Organizations like the Nature Conservancy and the Trust for Public Land help buy and protect precious lands in the United States and abroad. The Center for Ecosystem Survival does the same for rain forests and coral reefs. Forward-looking nations create parks and sanctuaries. This can work. In late 2000, scientists determined the most important biodiversity "hot spots" in the world—places that, if saved, will preserve the greatest amount of diversity in the smallest amount of land.

4. Environmental problems don't affect me personally. Everyone is potentially impacted by smoggy air, polluted water, contaminated fish, and water shortages—and even more by certain food choices. A high-calorie diet of meat, dairy, and fat can contribute to a long list of diseases, especially if the foods are grown with a lot of pesticides, antibiotics, and hormones. These same food choices harm the planet. In addition, your job, your money, and your morale are impacted by environmental issues.

5. Governments, businesses, and scientists will find all the solutions we need. Even if they could, the participation of individuals is vital. Individuals are the ultimate purchasers. Corporations do what they do because we buy their products. Governments have many other tasks to fulfill and typically meet stiff resistance when they try to create or enforce environmental regulations. Some industries fight regulations every step of the way, corrupt the agencies created to enforce them, ship jobs overseas to countries with laxer laws, and find other ways to dodge environmental responsibility. Automakers, meatpackers, chemical companies, fast food chains and some other industries have traditionally put profits before people and planet. Corporate executives make political contributions, hire public relations firms to distort facts, and fund carefully researched advertisements to manipulate us into buying their products while ignoring their dangers. Fortunately, a few companies are beginning to do more than laws require and finding innovative ways to be good citizens of the earth.

Governments need popular support to carry out their regulatory role. Regulations can work to save the earth. For instance, chlorofluorocarbons were banned over industry's dire warnings and protests, yet we have survived perfectly well without them. Air and water quality are improved when we pass and enforce laws making pollution illegal. But because big corporations and special interest groups make massive contributions to politicians, they influence legislation. The current federal administration has undone advances made by previous administrations, decided to drill in the arctic, abandoned the Kyoto Treaty (one of the few global environmental treaties), and done everything in its power to speed up the liquidation of earth.

Scientists know what we need to do. Though the numbers aren't perfect, we know that the answer is to save habitats, consume less, and reduce overpopulation. It's unrealistic to think that scientists will be able to create something out of nothing, or to find endless supplies for consumerism. Materials and energy have to come from somewhere.

The authors of this book believe that

- Earth cannot support infinite numbers of people living luxurious lifestyles; therefore, we need some restraint on consumption and population;

- Power and money tempt some people to dominate and impoverish others, hogging natural resources; therefore, some laws and regulations are needed;
- Market forces and technology do have creative power; therefore, innovation should be encouraged;
- Pragmatic solutions, emanating from synthesizers and applied locally, do work; therefore, we can have hope.

The solution is individual participation. We individuals can participate in saving the earth. But there are so many points of view, so many conflicting facts. How can we reconcile them? If experts think there is a danger but don't agree on the exact extent of it, we recommend the precautionary principle: better safe than sorry.

Do we need nature?

Biosphere II was a $200 million experiment in creating a self-contained habitat. During the 1990s, an elaborate enclosed mini-world was constructed with the input of dedicated scientists, in the hope of providing a human-made ecosystem within which animals, plants, and humans could live. It failed in less than a year, unable to sustain eight people. Now think of building a human colony on the moon. The colonists would have to create their own air, water, and temperature. Without healthy soil, plants, and oceans to cushion temperature extremes, the earth would be as inhospitable as the moon. We would freeze or roast without earth's blanket of soil, trees, and plants. We would starve if bees and other creatures didn't pollinate our crops. Nature's services like these are worth $36 trillion a year, but earth gives them to us for free. In fact, we can't even create a world for a few people, as Biosphere II showed.

Dueling data: Trade-offs and debates

Environmental issues are complex. Scientists continue to discover new interrelationships in nature and the impacts they have. There are changing cultural trends, new products, new technologies, new lists of endangered species—it's impossible to know everything. Even if you're right today, you may be wrong tomorrow. Solutions can be complex, too. An invention may solve one problem but create another one.

Reputable scientists and scientific organizations such as the EPA, the World Wildlife Federation, the Union of Concerned Scientists, and the Intergovernmental Panel on Climate Change agree that global warming and other environmental threats exist. Less clear are the exact causes and solutions. Experts don't always agree about these. A discovery, procedure, or recommendation made sincerely by one researcher or activist may be criticized just as sincerely by another. They may be looking at different sets of data, or interpreting the data differently, or considering different scales of systems, or different time scales.

Take this example. In a certain pond, water lily plants double in volume every day. On the first day, they cover only 1 percent of the pond. The next day, there are twice as many plants, but they still cover only 2 percent of the pond. Question: How much time is there between the time the pond is half covered by the plants, and when it is completely covered? Answer: one day. This is only a metaphor, but it reminds us that problems that grow exponentially can become very serious very quickly. Historians and archeologists have found that throughout history people have depleted and destroyed their own habitats. We must be careful not to do it again on a global scale.

Trade-offs occur when good intentions compete against hard realities or against other good intentions. For example, plastics are lightweight, flexible, and convenient. But they are made of fossil fuel and other chemicals, are dangerous to those working in or living near factories, cause illness in humans and death in animals, and do not really degrade. For another example, we recommend buying food grown near you to minimize the costs of refrigerating and transporting. Yet we also encourage you to try diverse foods, some of which may have been grown far away. This apparent contradiction can be resolved if we create a local market for something that was originally exotic, such as kiwis and Braeburn apples, which are now grown locally.

Some trade-offs will be solved as we learn how to balance the many elements of nature. Others may not be easily solved, and we'll have to live with them. Many bright ideas involve trade-offs or go through a stage of criticism and debate. That's normal and to be expected. So when you read in the news that a certain good idea has critics, don't be surprised. Stay tuned, watch out for greenwash, and beware of misleading public relations ploys.

Another way you can respond to the complex issues is to choose the least harmful option. You may not have time to investigate every consumer issue, but you can adopt the precautionary principle: better safe than sorry. For example, it's probably wise to limit your exposure to the thousands of toxic chemicals that have not been fully tested for human safety.

Environmental problems are serious and demand urgent action, but we must be able to communicate constructively about them. Here are six reasons:

- Nature is vast and complicated. Scientists are still working out the details of the complex webs of each ecosystem. The reduction or extinction of one species has ripple effects we are just beginning to understand. No one has all the answers.

- Actions taken with the best of intentions may lead to undesirable outcomes that no one predicted. A solution in one generation (such as the invention of pesticides) becomes a problem in the next (pollution of soil and water, and harm to our bodies). This is the law of unintended consequences.

- Seeking perfect knowledge and perfect solutions can delay us from using solutions that are "good enough." Perfectionism can undermine motivation and delay action.

- Simple error and ignorance account for so much of the environmental danger that it isn't necessary to see others as enemies, even though callous and greedy people and institutions do exist. There's enough for all of us to do even if we concentrate only on positive actions we agree on. As scientists, activists, regulators, and inventors diagnose and treat our ailing earth, each one of us can contribute by taking the actions we believe in.

- There's a range of roles with different time frames. Some people respond to emergencies while others engage in long-range strategies or inventions. Both are needed.
- Some solutions require trade-offs. We'll need to refine our skill in balancing competing interests and learn to live with imperfect answers.

"The sustainability movement does not agree on everything, nor should it ever. But remarkably, it shares a basic set of fundamental understandings about the earth and how it functions, and about the necessity of fairness and equity for all people in partaking of the earth's life-giving systems. This shared understanding is arising spontaneously from different economic sectors, cultures, regions, and cohorts."

Business guru and ecologist Paul Hawken

What you can do:

✓ Learn about both sides of a debate.

✓ Be alert for greenwash.

✓ Reduce or eliminate consumption of products that you have doubts about.

✓ Respect honest efforts to be sustainable even though they may not be perfect.

✓ Write to manufacturers, advertisers, elected officials, and regulators.

✓ Remember that your actions do have an impact.

Sustainable agriculture

Farmers, scientists, voluntary associations, and university programs are working to develop ways to grow food with minimal damage to the earth. The movement is called sustainable agriculture. Its main features include the following:

- No-till technology. Sustainable farmers plant with no-till drills and careful monitoring. This means less chemical use, less erosion, better water filtration, and more soil diversity.

- Natural solutions to pests. Sustainable farmers rotate crops, plant native grasses under trees, let natural predators handle pests, and tolerate a few harmless weeds.

- Integrated pest management. This is a carefully developed system
of handling insects and weeds. Instead of blanketing the land with huge sprays of chemicals, the farmer uses natural solutions, with chemicals only as a last resort.

- Rotating crops with animals. Animals are brought in to churn up the soil, deposit fertilizer, and eliminate pests. Goats, for example, may be brought in to eat weeds and geese to eat insects.

- Agro-forestry. Trees are planted with other crops growing below. The crop produces a regular income for the landowner while the trees are growing large enough to sell for lumber and pulp.

Modern agriculture, with huge fields of identical crops, attracts pests by giving them a plentiful and predictable food supply. It then applies pesticides to get rid of them. Modern livestock management is very damaging to soil, water, and air. Both systems are implemented without due regard for the human needs of farmers and their communities. By contrast, sustainable agriculture looks at the whole picture. It blends production efficiency, economic viability, social responsibility, and environmental compatibility.

Some food companies are working directly with farmers to promote sustainability. For example, Odwalla, Stonyfield Farms, Wild Oats, and Eden Foods cultivate a roster of organic farmers. Some pro-

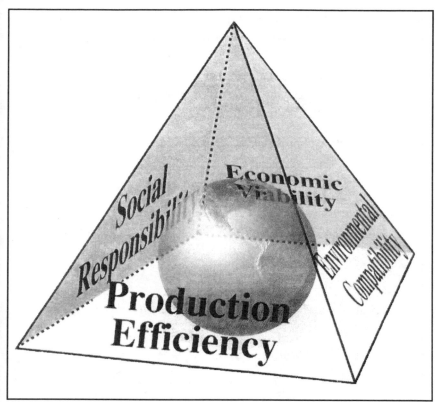

Pyramid diagram reprinted by permission of the Ohio State University College of Food, Agriculture, and Environmental Sciences.

ducers and retailers are even more active, offering small farmers loans, education, cooperation, and the knowledge that they aren't alone.

In fact, sustainable farmers are part of a growing movement. In the largest study of sustainable agriculture (surveying 200 projects in 52 countries), researchers found that sustainable agriculture exists in 3 percent of the world's fields, increasing yields 40 to 100 percent and helping the poorest farmers. No-till methods save labor, raise yields, improve soil quality, and help keep carbon in the ground instead of in the atmosphere. In fact, in the struggle to contain greenhouse gases, no-till agriculture creates a carbon credit.

Organic methods can sometimes outperform conventional ones. One study found that Washington apples grown organically not only tasted better, they were also more profitable. Water efficiency can also be improved; computers help calculate how much water a plant needs and is getting, precisely aiming sprinklers. Excessive use of pesticides and other earth-damaging practices could be made obsolete by making small changes in timing or placing seeds, and growing plants in beneficial pairings. And when food is grown without tons of chemicals, which can drift on the wind or leach into creeks and groundwater, people can live nearby. This allows farmers to coexist with suburbanites.

> "Unlike industrial agriculture, which looks at the farm as an outdoor factory with inputs entering at one end and outputs exiting the other, sustainable agriculture views a farm as an integrated system made up of elements like soil, plants, insects, and animals."

Michael Brower and Warren Leon of the Union of Concerned Scientists

What you can do:

- ✓ Buy organic.
- ✓ Pay attention to various green seals (labels indicating food is grown sustainably).
- ✓ Grow some of your own food.
- ✓ Learn about permaculture and biodynamic farming.
- ✓ Investigate sustainable agriculture and community supported agriculture.

Cruelty and animal living conditions

You may assume that the cows, pigs, and chickens destined for our tables live decent lives in farms regulated by somebody and that they are subjected to a quick and painless death. Sad to say, it's not true. Billions of cows, chickens, and pigs still live in appalling conditions in factory farms.

Chickens are raised in cages in warehouses with thousands of other birds. Veterinarian Michael Fox tells us, "There is not enough room for the hens to lie down, fluff their feathers, or even stretch their wings. Because of the cramped conditions, chickens become crazed, pecking one another severely, sometimes to death." So the chickens' beaks are cut off with a hot knife, which causes pain for weeks. Some chickens can't eat as a result, and they starve. Each survivor lives in about one square foot of space. They're given antibiotics and other drugs to keep them alive long enough to sell. According to Bernard Rollin, it is "more economically efficient to put a greater number of birds into each cage, accepting lower productivity per bird but greater productivity per cage. . . . chickens are cheap, cages are expensive."

To produce a single egg, a battery hen must live in a tiny cage for 24 hours. "Forced molting" means starving the hens of food and water for up to 18 days, which paradoxically causes them to produce more eggs. Between 5 and 10 percent die during this process. Male chicks, considered economically useless, are gassed or ground up alive—280 million of them a year.

Cattle spend the last weeks of their lives in feedlots, where they are fattened on a diet of corn and soybeans. They are herded together in pens with no shade or room to move. Disease is rampant; cattle are given antibiotics to fight the diseases, and more antibiotics in case they get other diseases (a procedure that helps make bacteria resistant to antibiotics), and growth hormones as well. Former rancher Howard Lyman says, "In those days, I never met a chemical I didn't like."

Dairy cows are bred, drugged, and kept continuously pregnant to produce much more milk than nature intended, which leaves their udders painfully distended and subject to infection. In 1967, a typical cow made 9,000 pounds of milk a year. Today, she produces almost 16,000 pounds—nearly twice as much. This exhausts her system, leaving her vulnerable to deficiency diseases. Dairy cows can live up to 25 years, but modern factory dairy farming uses them up in four or five years and then sends them to slaughter.

And what about calves raised for veal? They live in almost complete isolation, in narrow crates with not enough room to walk, turn around, or comfortably lie down. Their liquid diet is spiked with antibiotics and is low in iron to keep their flesh pale.

Pigs live in small cages all their lives, some scarcely bigger than their bodies. Most producers allow only three to five square feet per pig, plus space for feed and waste in the pen. The hog industry's own reports indicate that 70 percent of confined hogs suffer painful foot and leg infections, skin mange, and chronic respiratory diseases. No anesthetics are given for ear tagging, tail amputation, or castration. Robert Kennedy, Jr. studied the issue and he found that "Stadium-sized warehouses shoehorn a hundred thousand sows into claustrophobic cages that hold them in one position for a lifetime over metal-grate floors. Below, aluminum culverts collect and channel their putrefying waste into ten-acre, open-air pits three stories deep from which miasmal vapors choke surrounding communities and tens of millions of gallons of hog feces ooze into North Carolina's rivers."

- Each year, 200,000 pigs are unfit for human consumption largely due to handling or transport, 80,000 just from the crowding.

- Animals are often not fed in their last days because the food would not have time to be turned into meat and the producers can avoid the expense.

- "Downers" are animals so debilitated by their lives and transport that they can't stand up. It is legal to drag them into the slaughterhouse and kill them for human food, but some of them are simply left in the yards to die slowly, abandoned because it's not worth the time or vet bill to help them. "Dead piles" therefore accumulate outside slaughterhouses.

- Poultry is exempt from laws requiring that animals be stunned before slaughter. The animals are seized by the feet and hung upside down on conveyor belts to the din of hundreds of other bellowing and thrashing animals.

- Four meatpacking firms control 84 percent of the slaughtering industry in this country, and eight poultry firms control two thirds of the poultry business.

> "For modern animal agriculture, the less the consumer knows what's about happening before the meat hits the plate, the better. If true, is this an ethical situation? Should we be reluctant to let people know what really goes on, because we're not really proud of it and concerned that it might turn them to vegetarianism?"
>
> *Peter Cheeke, professor of animal agriculture*

Some good news

Fortunately, there is some good news. Thanks in part to efforts by caring activists, in mid-2000 McDonald's announced it would begin to require their suppliers to treat animals more humanely. Practices such as starving the hens of food and water, debeaking them, or crowding them into less than 72 square inches of living space each will be discontinued. Another good development is the "farmed free" seal devised by the United States Department of Agriculture and the Humane Association. To earn this seal, farmers must eliminate cages for laying hens and stop forced molting. Cattle must have access to pastures. The new USDA organic label applies to meat animals, which must have access to pasture and no antibiotics.

What you can do

✓ If you eat meat, pay attention to the emerging green seals. When farmed-free food comes to your area, support it.

✓ If you eat meat, buy USDA organic meat.

✓ Write to your congressperson protesting cruelty on factory farms.

✓ Let McDonald's know you approve of their changes and would appreciate any additional moves to improve animals' lives.

✓ Don't invest in cruel agribusiness, or if you do, exercise your shareholder rights to protest these horrors.

✓ If you sincerely want to improve the lot of animals, you could eat less of them—or none at all.

Growing Your Food

Growing food can be rewarding in many ways. Most of them help the earth:

- You experience the creativity of helping something grow.
- If you use no chemicals, you know that what you've grown is organic.
- You can promote biodiversity by selecting varieties that agribusinesses don't grow.
- In your small plot, you won't cause the problems of monoculture.
- You can avoid genetically modified foods.
- No packaging, refrigerating, or gasoline are used to transport the food, though your first batch of seeds and fertilizer probably did get trucked.
- A vegetable garden is the perfect place to use the compost you've been faithfully making.

"During World War II, many Americans planted 'victory gardens.' These gardens supplied families with food at a crucial point in our national history. We still need victory gardens, this time, to combat the environmental crisis and regenerate the earth. . . Nature, left to its own devices, usually heals itself. As organic gardeners and healers of the earth, we should allow this self-regeneration to happen, and we should also assist the process where the natural healing capacity has been diminished by pollution."

Robert and Maria Rodale,
publishers of books about nature, cooking, and gardening.

Growing food does take time, but maybe less than you think. A 10-gallon pot with one tomato plant could yield 20 pounds of tomatoes and requires only a few minutes a week. Three zucchini plants could yield 15 to 20 pounds. Did you know that gardening is America's No.1 hobby? At least 72 million households participated in gardening in 1995. Two-thirds of American households have at least one gardener, and they spend $27 billion. Growing food supports self-sufficiency and freedom of choice. Within the conditions of your climate, you can grow the food you like. You can cook and preserve the food you like. It will taste better than store-bought and commercially grown food because you made it. Science teacher and avid gardener Andy Snow says, "If you perceive gardening as work, it will seem like work, making it harder to persevere until you see the payoffs. But if you see gardening as a labor of love, an alternative to the stationary bikes at the athletic club, a spiritual reconnection to the productive cycles of our earth, an opportunity to heal a little patch of land, it is a success by any measure."

If your community doesn't have a group, start one

In San Francisco, at a project for the homeless called Fresh Start Farms, Ruth Brinker helps these unemployed people grow food on a small plot with biointensive methods. In another program, inmates in the county jail can participate in the Garden Project, which was founded in 1984 by Catherine Sneed, giving food they grow to soup kitchens and AIDS patients. The Garden Project now employs 35 people and works 12 acres. When released from incarceration, participants can join a project to grow food for a restaurant and bakery.

In St. Louis, children called Earth Angels have a multi-faceted program of their own. 150 kids age 6 to12 in four neighborhood groups grow food. Eight of their sites are also certified by the National Wildlife Federation's Backyard Habitat Program. In the last dozen years they have also picked up and recycled 250,000 aluminum cans, 30 tons of glass, 6 tons of newspaper, 1,500 tires, and more. The Earth Angels have donated over $1,000 to save ancient forests and $1,400 to save tapirs in Ecuador.

In Food from the Hood, which started in Los Angeles in 1992, high school students own and run the business of growing food. They earn money for scholarships, donate 25 percent of the crop to the needy, and sell their salad dressings and applesauce to 2,000 stores.

In Hawaii, a small group of families decided to revive the almost-vanished cultivation of taro, a root at the heart of traditional Hawaiian diet and culture. Reconnecting youth to elders, a cultural center teaches botany and ecology. With help from the Trust for Public Land, a breathtaking valley threatened by development was saved to revive taro traditions that go back a thousand years.

What you can do

✓ Start with something that's likely to succeed. You can buy kits with pots, soil, instructions, and already planted seeds. As you gain experience, branch out.

✓ Get seeds from a gardening or hardware store, by mail order, or over the Internet.

✓ Better yet, contact a seed preservation organization and plant some heirloom varieties.

✓ Practice growing food by volunteering at a community supported agriculture farm.

✓ Consult the public library for books on the subject.

Community gardening groups exist to help you. Find those active in your community or you could contact the Center for Urban Education about Sustainable Agriculture. In community gardens, citizens join together to plant and tend gardens for food and beauty. Some food co-ops have such a garden as one of their programs. These experiences build community, well-being, and a healthier earth.

In California, the Berkeley Center for Ecoliteracy got a grant from the USDA to help high schools grow organic food. Twelve of the district's 15 schools have organic gardens and in 1999, the Berkeley school board passed a resolution to ensure that all the district's 10,000 students get some organic food at lunch. Another group, the Berkeley Community Gardening Collaborative, affiliated with Americorps, California Conservation Corps, the city of Berkeley, Chez Panisse, and other organizations, conducts community gardening, youth training, and mentoring in at-risk neighborhoods.

Besides cooking and eating your produce, you can also swap it with friends and neighbors for their produce, creating your own mini-economy, or share it with food banks. And you can sell it. Some restaurants not only grow some of their own vegetables and herbs, they also partner with local micro-gardeners.

You could revive the old kitchen arts of preserving and canning. Homemade pickles and applesauce can be great fund-raisers for church groups and clubs. Make your own jam, your own vinegar, even your own wine and beer. The possibilities for creativity and community are great.

Some final thoughts

All kinds of people are taking part in the shift to earth-friendly living: students, architects, homemakers, activists, legislators, doctors, surfers, Internet designers, artists, chefs, school children.... Some love nature, some are devoted to social justice, some care about animals, some are concerned about the world they are leaving to their children and grandchildren. Spiritual values motivate many of us, whether we call it earth stewardship, religious environmentalism, or green spirituality. Others find creative and economic opportunity, as new inventions and services are called for.

The producers of food (both small farms and forward-looking agricultural interests) are developing earth-friendly methods of growing your food. Distributors (regional alliances of growers, health food stores, and increasingly, some large supermarket chains) are making it available. Now it is up to you, the consumer, to encourage them by buying with the earth in mind.

In this book, you've read about children collecting money to save rainforests, farmers discovering how to grow food sustainably, automakers beating their own goals of waste reduction, office workers saving trees, inventors discovering ways to replace plastic, coffee growing that helps birds, and successes in growing earth-friendly food. You've discovered that you can help, one meal at a time. Perhaps you'll be inspired to do even more.

Please send your success stories and ideas to our website (*www.savenature.org/food*) so we can share them. There's no limit to the ways your creativity, inventiveness, and love of planet and people can help save the earth.

Bluebirds and rainforests

For years, children in Homestead School, Glen Spey, New York, have sent money to the Center for Ecosystem Survival, which protects rainforests and coral reefs. One year the director learned the children wanted to save the Eastern bluebirds in their own backyard, which were threatened from loss of habitat. So the children built and sold birdhouses for the bluebirds to live in, and sent the proceeds to the Center for Ecosystem Survival. In the last six years, the children of Homestead School have contributed almost $40,000 to saving 400 acres of rainforest.

A Few Good Books

Ausubel, Kenny. (1997). *Restoring the Earth: Visionary Solutions from the Bioneers.* Tiburon, CA: H J Kramer.

Berrill, Michael. (1997). *The Plundered Seas: Can the World's Fish Be Saved?* San Francisco: Sierra Club Books.

Brower, Michael, and Warren Leon. (1999). *The Consumer's Guide to Effective Environmental Choices.* NY: Three Rivers Press.

Council on Economic Priorities. (2000). *Shopping for a Better World: The Quick and Easy Guide to All Your Socially Responsible Shopping.* SF. Sierra Club Books.

Fox, Michael W. (1997). *Eating with Conscience: The Bioethics of Food.* Troutdale, OR: New Sage Press.

Haas, Elson M. (1999). *The Staying Healthy Shopper's Guide: Feed Your Family Safely.* Berkeley: Celestial Arts.

Hawken, Paul. (1993). *The Ecology of Commerce: A Declaration of Sustainability.* NY: Harper Business.

Hawken, Paul, Amory Lovins and L. Hunter Lovins. (1999). *Natural Capitalism: Creating the Next Industrial Revolution.* Boston: Little, Brown.

Lilienfeld, Robert, and William Rathje. (1998). *Use Less Stuff: Environmental Solutions For Who We Really Are.* NY: Fawcett.

Lerner, Steve. (1997). *Eco-pioneers: Practical Visionaries Solving Today's Environmental Problems.* Cambridge: MIT Press.

Loeb, Paul Rogat. (1999). *Soul of a Citizen: Living with Conviction in a Cynical Time.* NY: St. Martin's Griffin.

Lyman, Howard, and G. Merzer (1998). *The Mad Cowboy: Plain Talk from the Cattle Rancher Who Won't Eat Meat.* NY: Scribner.

Marcus, Erik. (2000). *Vegan: The New Ethics of Eating.* Ithaca, NY: McBooks.

Meadows, Donella H., Dennis L. Meadows and Jorgen Randers. (1992). *Beyond the Limits: Confronting Global Collapse, Envisioning a Sustainable Future.* White River Junction, VT: Chelsea Green.

Ray, Paul H., and Sherry Ruth Anderson. (2001). *The Cultural Creatives: How 50 Million People Are Changing the World.* Easton, PA: Harmony Press.

Robbins, John. (1987). *Diet for a New America.* Tiburon: H J Kramer.

Robbins, John. (2001). *The Food Revolution.* Berkeley, CA: Conari.

Ryan, John C. (1999). *Seven Wonders: Everyday Things for a Healthier Planet.* San Francisco: Sierra Club Books.

Ryan, John C., and Durning, Alan T. (1997). *Stuff: The Secret Life of Everyday Things.* Seattle: Northwest Environment Watch.

Shapiro, Howard-Yana and John Harrisson. (2000). *Gardening for the Future of the Earth.* NY: Bantam.

See our website (www.savenature.org/food) for valuable organizations and sources for our facts.